COGNITIVE BEHAVIORAL THERAPY MADE SIMPLE

Strategies for Change Your Life in 21 Days, The Most Effective Methods to Overcoming & Manage Anxiety, Depression, Panic and Negative Thought Patterns.

TABLE OF CONTENTS

INTRODUCTION

Cognitive behavior therapy is a brain science discipline that looks to help individuals adapt to dysfunctional emotions. Unlike different kinds of open-ended therapy, cognitive behavior therapy is goal-situated and efficient. This kind of therapy is regularly utilized for treating mood disorders, anxiety disorders, psychological disorders, substance abuse, and dietary problems. Furthermore, the therapy has been demonstrated as being successful for a portion of the populace in treating post-traumatic stress disorder, OCD, depression, and even specific disorders like bulimia nervosa.

As a result of the viability of CBT, it is generally an exceptionally short encounter, unlike some different types of therapy that can continue for quite a long time. CBT can be independently based or based within a meeting. As of late, more effort has been made to utilize CBT for treating lawbreakers in therapeutic settings. In these occurrences, therapists endeavor to correct criminal behavior via cognitive abilities and teach them ways of dealing with stress that will help decrease their criminal behavior.

In this procedure, therapists/doctors will identify and examine a patient's thoughts and beliefs. (These will be perceivable through a progression of tests) The goal is to decide how these beliefs are connected with crippling behavior, for example, alcohol abuse, criminal behavior, and so on. Cognitive behavior therapy was designed during the 1960s to blend the best of behavioral therapy results with that of cognitive therapy. While these two disciplines have different sources overall, they discovered a shared opinion when concentrating on treatment.

There are two fundamental parts to break down in this discipline, and they are additionally the two principle speculations at work: cognitive and behavioral. If you experience the ill effects of social anxiety disorder, however, and would prefer not to explore the choices of medication, at that point, cognitive behavior therapy is a brilliant option. It is as of now considered the best way of treating social anxiety disorder, and it is undeniably progressively as effective as using ;just medication alone.

CHAPTER ONE
WHAT CONSTITUTES COGNITIVE BEHAVIORAL THERAPY?

Cognitive-behavioral therapy is a psychotherapeutic approach that expects to show individuals new abilities as to the best way to take care of issues concerning dysfunctional emotions, behaviors, and comprehensions through an objective, arranged, systematic approach. This title is utilized from numerous points of view to characterize behavioral therapy; cognitive therapy; and therapy that depends on the behavioral and cognitive treatments.

There is observational proof that demonstrates cognitive-behavioral therapy is very successful in treating several conditions, including character, anxiety, state of mind, overeating, substance abuse, and maniacal disorders. Treatment is frequently manualized, as specific mental requests are treated with specific technique-driven brief, direct, and time-constrained medicines.

Cognitive-behavioral therapy can be utilized both with individuals and in meetings. The techniques are frequently adjusted for self-improvement sessions too. It is up to the individual clinician or specialist on whether he/she is increasingly cognitive arranged, progressively behavioral situated, or a mix of both, as each of the three strategies is utilized today.

Cognitive-behavioral therapy resulted from a blend of behavioral therapy and cognitive therapy. These two treatments have numerous differences, yet discovered a shared opinion on concentrating on the "present time and place" and on mitigating manifestations.

Assessing cognitive behavioral therapy has prompted many to accept that it is progressively more powerful than psychodynamic medications and other different strategies. The United Kingdom advocates the utilization of cognitive-behavioral therapy over different strategies for some types of psychological wellness difficulties, including post-traumatic distress disorder, fanatical compulsive disorder, bulimia nervosa, clinical depression, and the neurological condition perpetual weakness disorder/myalgic encephalomyelitis.

The forerunners of cognitive-behavioral therapy base their underlying foundations in different antiquated philosophical customs, particularly Stoicism. The advanced foundations of CBT can be tracked to the improvement of behavioral therapy during the 1920s, the improvement of cognitive therapy during the 1960s, and the consequent converging of the two treatments. The principal behavioral remedial approaches were circulated in 1924 by Mary Cover Jones, whose work brought about the unlearning of phobias in youngsters.

The new behavioral approaches worked well with a considerable amount of the hypochondriac disorders, yet less with depression. Behavioral therapy was likewise losing in prominence due to the "cognitive unrest." This,

4

in the long run, prompted cognitive therapy being established by Aaron T. Beck during the 1960s. Arnold A. Lazarus created the primary type of cognitive-behavioral therapy during the timespan of the late 1950s through the 1970s.

During the 1980s and 1990s, cognitive and behavioral treatments were joined by work done by David M. Clark in the United Kingdom and David H. Barlow in the United States. Cognitive-behavioral therapy incorporates the accompanying frameworks: cognitive therapy, reasonable emotive behavior therapy, and multimodal therapy. Probably the best test is characterizing precisely what cognitive-behavioral therapy is. The specific helpful techniques change inside the different approaches of CBT, relying on whatever sort of issues are being managed. However, the methods are generally based on the following:

- Keeping a journal of significant occasions and related sentiments, thoughts, and behaviors.

- Addressing and testing insights, assessments, suspicions, and convictions that may be ridiculous and unhelpful.

- Step by step confronting exercises that may have been maintained a strategic distance from.

- Evaluating better approaches for carrying on and responding.

What's more, diversion techniques, care, and relaxing are additionally generally utilized in cognitive behavioral therapy. Mind-set settling drugs are additionally regularly combined with treatments to treat conditions like bipolar disorder. The NICE rules inside the British NHS see cognitive behavioral therapy's application in treating schizophrenia in a mixture with prescription drugs and therapy.

Cognitive-behavioral therapy ordinarily sets aside effort for patients to successfully actualize it into their lives. It more often than not requires concentrated exertion for them to supplant a dysfunctional cognitive-emotional behavioral procedure or propensity with a progressively sensible and versatile one, notwithstanding when they see when and where their psychological methods go astray.

Cognitive-behavioral therapy is connected to a wide range of circumstances, including the following conditions:

Anxiety disorders (excessive compulsive disorder, social fear or social anxiety, generalized anxiety disorder)

State of mind disorders (clinical depression, major depressive disorder, mental indications)

A sleeping disorder (counting being more compelling than the medication Zopiclone)

Extreme mental disorders (schizophrenia, bipolar disorder, serious depression)

Kids and young people (major depressive disorder, anxiety disorders, injury and post-traumatic stress disorder side effects)

Stammering (to enable them to defeat anxiety, shirking behaviors, and negative thoughts about themselves)

Cognitive-behavioral therapy includes showing an individual new ways to beat dysfunctional emotions, behaviors, and discernments through an objective situated, systematic approach. There is exact proof demonstrating cognitive-behavioral therapy is successful in treating numerous conditions, including excessive compulsive disorder, generalized anxiety disorder, major depressive disorder, schizophrenia, anxiety, and negative thoughts about oneself). With the tremendous measure of accomplishment seen by the utilization of this therapy, it is one of the most significant apparatuses that scientists and specialists need to treat mental disorders today.

Cognitive-Behavioral Therapy - The Basics

Cognitive-Behavioral Therapy is a type of psychotherapy that underscores the significant role of thinking, by the way we feel and act.

Cognitive-behavioral therapy does not exist as an unmistakable helpful procedure. The expression "cognitive-behavioral therapy (CBT)" is an extended-term for classification of treatments with similarities. There are several ways to deal with cognitive-behavioral therapy, but, most cognitive-behavioral treatments have the accompanying qualities:

1 - CBT is organized and orderly.

Cognitive-behavioral therapists have a specific motivation for each session. Specific systems/ideas are taught during each session. CBT centers around the client's goals. We don't tell our clients what their goals "should" be, or what they "should" endure. We are mandated as in we tell our clients the best way to think and act via various tactics to get what they need. In this manner, CBT therapists don't instruct their clients - instead, they show their clients what to do.

2 - CBT is a synergistic exertion between the therapist and the client.

Cognitive-behavioral therapists try to determine what their clients genuinely desire (their objectives) and afterward help their clients accomplish those objectives. The therapist's job is to tune in, educate, and support, while the client's responsibilities are to express their concerns, learn, and execute that knowledge.

3 – Homework is a focal element of CBT.

If when you endeavored to gain proficiency with your multiplication tables you went through just a single hour of the week examining them, you may even now be pondering what 5 X 5 equals. You probably invested a lot of energy at home studying your multiplication tables, perhaps with cheat sheets.

The equivalent is the situation with psychotherapy. Scientific accomplishment (if acquired) could take an exceptionally prolonged period if each of them as an individuals were to consider the procedures and themes instructed were only used for one hour out of every week. That is why CBT therapists relegate perusing assignments and urge their clients to rehearse the methods being learned.

4 - CBT utilizes the Socratic Method

The Cognitive-behavioral therapists need to pick up an excellent comprehension of their clients' worries. That is why they regularly pose inquiries. They additionally urge their clients to raise queries about themselves, similar to, "How would I truly realize that those people are giggling at me?" or "Might they be laughing about something different?

5 - CBT depends on a separate way of thinking.

Not all ways to deal with CBT emphasize detachment. Rational Emotive Behavior Therapy, Rational Behavior Therapy, and Rational Living Therapy stress apathy. Beck's Cognitive Therapy did not depend on taboos. Cognitive-behavioral therapy does not tell people how they should feel. In any case, the vast majority looking for therapy would prefer not to feel the way they have been feeling.

The methodologies that stress detachment shows the advantages of feeling, even from a pessimistic standpoint, quiet when going up against undesirable situations. They additionally underscore the way we handle our unwanted situations whether we are vexed about them or not. If we are annoyed about our problems, we have two issues - the problem, and our anger about it.

A great many people need to have the least number of

issues conceivable. So when we figure out how to more peacefully acknowledge an individual problem, in addition to the fact that we feel better, yet we, for the most part, have placed ourselves in a superior position to utilize our insight, learning, vitality, and assets to determine the problem.

6 - CBT depends on the Cognitive Model of Emotional Response.

Cognitive-behavioral therapy depends on the possibility that our contemplations cause our feelings and behaviors, not outside things, such as people, situations, and occasions. The advantage of this reality is we can change how we think to feel/act better regardless of whether the status changes or not.

7 - CBT depends on an instructive model.

CBT depends on the scientifically upheld suspicion that most passionate and behavioral responses are found out. Along these lines, the objective of therapy is to enable clients to unlearn their undesirable responses and to gain proficiency with another method for responding. Subsequently, CBT has nothing to do with "simply talking." People can "simply talk" with anybody. The instructive accentuation of CBT has an extra advantage - it prompts long term results. When people see how and why they are getting along well, they recognize what to do to keep progressing nicely.

8 - CBT is Time Limited and Briefer.

Cognitive-behavioral therapy was recognized in between the quickest regarding outcomes acquired. The usual number of sessions clients get (over a wide range of problems and the ways to deal with CBT) is just 16. Different types of therapy, like psychoanalysis, can take years. What empowers CBT to be briefer is its profoundly educational nature and the way it utilizes homework assignments.

CBT is time-restricted in that we help clients comprehend at the absolute beginning of the therapy process that there will be a moment when the formal therapy will end. The consummation of formal therapy is a choice made by the therapist and client. Along these lines, CBT isn't an open-ended, continual process.

9 - CBT hypothesis and procedures depend on the Inductive Method.

A focal part of rational thinking is that it depends on actuality. Frequently, we upset ourselves about things when the truth is told, and the situation doesn't turn out the way we think it should. If we realized that, we would not squander our time annoying ourselves. In this manner, the inductive technique urges us to take a look at our contemplations as being theories or conjectures that can be addressed and tried. If we find that our speculations are off base (since we have new data), at that point we can change our thinking to one that follows the true situation.

10 - A sound helpful relationship is vital for powerful therapy,

however, it's not the core interest. A few types of therapy accept that the primary reason people show signs of improvement in therapy is a direct result of the constructive connection between the therapist and client. Cognitive-behavioral therapists trust it is essential to have a decent relationship where one can confide in each other, yet that isn't sufficient. CBT therapists accept that the clients change since they figure out how to think differently, and they follow up on that knowledge. Subsequently, CBT therapists center around showing rational self-directing abilities.

The History of Cognitive Behavioral Therapy

Cognitive-behavioral therapy is an approach utilized by psychotherapists to impact a patient's behaviors and feelings. The way this method works is in its methodology, which must be deliberate. It has been used effectively to treat an assortment of disorders, including dietary problems, substance misuse, tension, and character disorders. It tends to be utilized in individuals or meeting style therapy sessions, and the approach can likewise be outfitted towards self-improvement therapy.

Cognitive-behavioral therapy is a blend of conventional behavioral therapy and cognitive therapy. They are joined into a treatment that is centered around manifestation expulsion. The adequacy of the procedure can be determined based on its results. The more it is utilized, the more it has moved toward being recommended. It is presently used as the primary treatment technique for post traumatic distress disorder, obsessive compulsion disorder, depression, and bulimia.

Cognitive-behavioral therapy initially started to be utilized somewhere in the timeframe of between 1960 and 1970. It was a slow procedure of blending behavioral therapy techniques and cognitive therapy techniques. Behavioral therapy had been around since the 1920s; however, cognitive therapy was not presented until the 1960s. Very quickly, the advantages of joining it with behavioral therapy techniques were figured it out. Ivan Pavlov, with his experiments with dogs who salivated at the ringing of a bell, was among the most renowned of the behavioral research pioneers. Other pioneers in the field included John Watson and Clark Hull.

Rather than concentrating on breaking down the problem like Freud and the psychoanalysts did, cognitive behavioral therapy focused on taking out the manifestations. The thought is that if you take out the indications, you have disposed of the problem. This more straightforward approach was viewed as progressively compelling at getting to the current issue and helping patients to make advances all the more rapidly.

As an increasingly radical forceful treatment, behavioral techniques managed progressively extreme problems. The more evident and apparent the manifestations were, the simpler it was to target them and devise procedures to dispose of them. Behavioral therapy was not as fruitful at first with increasingly equivocal problems, for example, depression. This domain was found to be treated better with cognitive therapy techniques.

In numerous academic settings, the two therapy

techniques were utilized next to each other to look into the results. It didn't take long before the upsides of consolidating the two technologies turned out to be clear as a method for exploiting the qualities of each. David Barlow's work on frenzy disorder treatments gave the first solid case of the achievement of using the consolidated methodologies.

Cognitive-behavioral therapy is difficult to characterize in a concise definition since it covers such an expansive scope of subjects and techniques. It is really an umbrella definition for individual treatments specifically customized to the problems of a specific patient. So, the problem directs the specifics of the treatment.

However, there are some basic subjects and techniques. These incorporate having the patient keep a journal of significant occasions which they use to record the sentiments and behaviors they had in association with every occasion. This element is then utilized as a foundation to dissect and test the patient's capacity to assess the situation and build up a fitting enthusiastic reaction.

Negative feelings and behaviors are identified, just like the assessments and convictions that lead to them. An effort is then made to counter these convictions and assessments to demonstrate that the subsequent behaviors aren't right. Negative responses are disposed of, and the patient is shown a superior method to see and respond to the situation.

Some portion of the therapy likewise incorporates showing the patient approaches to occupy themselves or
14

change their concentration from something disquieting or a situation that is producing negative behavior. They figure out how to concentrate on something different rather than the negative upgrade, subsequently dispensing with the negative reaction that it would prompt.

The problem is checked from developing in any way. For certain mental disorders like bipolar disorder or schizophrenia, psychological medications are frequently endorsed to use along with these techniques. The prescriptions give the patient a satisfactory calming influence to offer them a chance to study the situation and make a solid decision when previously they couldn't stop to consider a more balanced idea.

Cognitive-behavioral therapy has been demonstrated as being compelling for an assortment of problems. However, it is as yet a procedure, not a miracle cure. It requires some investment to instruct patients to understand circumstances and identify the triggers of their negative behaviors. When this progression is successful, despite everything, it still requires a ton of exertion to defeat their first viewpoints and instead stop and make the correct decisions. First, they realize what they should do, and after that, they should rehearse until they can do it.

The Importance of Cognitive Behavior Therapy

In life, we need to confront many different sorts of

situations and additional others not all that appealing. How we live and whether we appreciate it or severely dislike it is an element of the sort of the point of view that we have just as the psychological makeups that we may pick up. There are some people who are constantly businesslike and furthermore, confident, which encourages them to meet all situations with courage and poise. On the other end of the scale, others are meek and additionally adversely inclined, which makes them very terrified, apprehensive and furthermore, frightened by every single thing.

While some people are fundamentally cynical in some other cases, people additionally experience horrible encounters that change their lives for eternity. For example, kids who witness a homicide or maybe a militant psychological assault could get damaged for life genuinely and be given to frenzy and anxiety attacks.

Some others likewise get harried and bothered to the degree they are perpetually despondent or possibly irritable and cranky and always angry. Regardless, these are generally instances of behaviorally dysfunctional actions and lifestyles that should be treated by methods of individual behavior therapy, which is otherwise called CBT.

CBT is a treatment whereby prepared specialists and guides sit with patients and attempt to enable them to discover for themselves the purpose behind why they act with a particular goal in mind. Thoughts offer a ride to the emotions and generate actions because of which it is fundamental to handle feelings and furthermore investigate them appropriately with the goal that the root cause of the issue might be separated and tended to. The primary method is to supplant negative thoughts with positive and cheerful ones until inspiration turns into a natural for the patient. This is the primary way one can end up healthy and upbeat indeed.

One ought not to accept that CBT is an essential strategy. For one, it needs a ton of careful and prolonged testing just as a mental treatment so the deep-rooted thoughts and incapacitating or might be made to blur away from plain sight. This will enable ecstasy to get to the frontal area and help an individual settle on decisions that are safe and healthy as well. Guarantee that life is lived to the fullest without any second thoughts.

What Benefits Can You Receive From Behavioral Therapy?

Behavioral therapy, otherwise called behavioral modification, is a way to deal with psychotherapy dependence on learning hypothesis that expects to treat psychopathology through methods intended to fortify wanted behaviors and dispose of undesired behaviors. Old-fashioned philosophical conventions, for example, Stoicism, provided the backgrounds of certain central parts of behavioral therapy.

The first use of the expression "behavioral therapy" may have been utilized in a 1953 research venture by B.F. Skinner, Ogden Lindsley, Nathan H. Azrin, and Harry C.

Solomon. Other early pioneers in this sort of therapy incorporate Joseph Wolpe and Hans Eysenck.

Behavioral therapy is considered to have three unmistakable starting points: South Africa (Wolpe's gathering), the United States (Skinner), and the United Kingdom (Rachman and Eysenck). Eysenck, specifically, saw behavioral problems as an interaction between condition, behavior, and individual qualities. Skinner's gathering, then again, took a more considerable amount of an operant conditioning approach, which included a practical way to deal with appraisal and intercessions concentrated on the possibility the board (reward and discipline for positive and negative behavior, separately, otherwise called the "token framework") and behavioral activation.

Skinner ended up keen on individualizing programs to improve the learning of individuals with and without handicaps; he worked with Fred S. Keller to create programmed guidance. Programmed guidance demonstrated clinical accomplishment in treating aphasia restoration. Skinner's understudy, Ogden Lindsley, is credited with shaping a development called "exactness instructing," which built up a diagramming program that monitored how much advancement the clients were making.

In the other 50% of the twentieth century, numerous therapists started consolidating this therapy with the cognitive therapy of Aaron Beck and Albert Ellis, which made up cognitive behavioral therapy. In certain territories, the cognitive part added to the therapy (particularly when it came to social fear treatment), yet in different zones, the cognitive segment did not add to the therapy. This prompted the quest for Third Generation Behavioral Therapies.

Third Generation Behavioral Therapies consolidates the essential standards of operant and respondent brain science with functional analysis and a Clinical detailing or case conceptualization of verbal behavior, which uses an enormous amount of the perspective on the behavioral investigators. Some exploration demonstrates that Third Generation Behavioral Therapies are more successful at times than cognitive therapy, yet more research should be done all together for the proof to be indisputable.

Probably the most generally utilized methodologies in behavioral therapy today incorporate Acceptance and Commitment Therapy (ACT), Cognitive Behavioral Analysis System of Psychotherapy (CBASP), behavioral activation (BA), and Integrative behavioral couples therapy. Behavioral therapy joins the standards of traditional conditioning created by Ivan Pavlov and the rules of operant conditioning created by B. F. Skinner. There has been some perplexity on how these two conditionings differ and how the different methods of this have any reasonable scientific premise. An online paper, "Fortifying Behavioral Therapy, gives a response to this perplexity.

Operant conditioning possibly encouraged the board programs. These programs have been very successful, even in adults who manage schizophrenia. Respondent conditioning has prompted precise desensitization and introduction and reaction avoidance. Social skills preparation shows clients the skills needed to reinforce and to decrease life discipline. Be that as it may, operant conditioning techniques in the meta-analysis had the best impact in preparing social skills. While social skills preparation had demonstrated some suitability for schizophrenia, applying behavioral programs to schizophrenia has commonly lost support among numerous therapists.

Behavioral therapy's center intercessions depend on functional analysis. Among the numerous problems that behavioral therapy have functionally broken down incorporate closeness in couples, forgiveness in couples, relationships, perpetual torment, anorexia, depression, weight, and anxiety. Functional analysis has even been connected to problems that therapists will regularly experience with patients, including regular clients, mostly drawn in clients, and client opposition. This has prompted impressive devices for therapists to use to upgrade supportive adequacy, including utilizing encouraging feedback or operant conditioning.

This has persuaded the world that behavioral therapy is as powerful, if not increasingly successful, for treating depression, attention-deficit hyperactivity disorder, and obsessive compulsive disorder than drug treatment. Another fruitful type of therapy that has shown incredible success is Habit inversion training. This has been demonstrated as being profoundly influential in treating tics.

The qualities of behavioral therapy incorporate being

experimental (information-driven), relevant (concentrating on condition and setting), functional (inspired by a behavior's result or impact), probabilistic (considering response to be measurably unsurprising), monistic (treating the individual as a unit and dismissing mind-body dualism), and social (investigating bidirectional communications).

Behavioral therapy created from three different purposes of beginning and has its foundations in both operant conditioning and respondent conditioning. Behavioral therapy has been demonstrated to be a viable, if not progressively more successful, than drug treatment when it comes to treating depression, attention-deficit hyperactivity disorder, and excessive compulsive disorder.

Third Generation Behavioral Therapies that are generally used to extraordinary impact today started from behavioral therapy. These are only a portion of the reasons why the revelation and improvement of behavioral therapy are so significant in our present reality.

CHAPTER TWO
UNDERSTANDING THE FUNDAMENTALS OF COGNITIVE BEHAVIOR THERAPY

Cognitive behavior therapy has been utilized to help patients who are suffering from depression, pressures, addictions, and a wide range of other psychosocial problems.

When undertaking cognitive behavior therapy, an expert encourages the suffering person to correct his thinking. It is accepted that thinking patterns and the way a person may see or identify with specific situations are associated with the patient's feelings and behavior.

Cognitive behavior therapy is a way to help find the primary reasons for the issue from a mental perspective and afterward change or right the thinking design that has prompted the wrong behavior.

Utilizing cognitive behavior therapy, an expert is attempting to modify the irrational and distorted thinking of the patient. This will assist the patient with making changes in their behavior and having the option to re-adjust it. Thinking patterns and feelings assume a crucial job in human behavior and can be changed or modified.

Cognitive behavior therapy is additionally used to help people with drug addictions, for example, cocaine. In the strictest sense of the word, people who turn to drugs, both legitimate physicians recommended medicines that are irresistible, just as unlawful drugs, could have a behavior issue and can gain from using cognitive behavior therapy.

There are an expanding number of people who are suffering from the useless issue and keeping in mind that some accept restorative medications might be sufficient. Studies appear to show that cognitive behavior therapy is effective. Much relies upon the person's readiness to consent to a trained therapist and to modify inward musings and emotions.

The trained therapist additionally is assisting the patient in comprehending past encounters and situations, via analyzing and learning not to respond in a silly or contorted way.

Cognitive behavior therapy has turned into a way of understanding the association between inward considerations and discernments and human behavior. This in no uncertain terms has added to some of the success that has been made. It likewise has helped a few people to make enormous changes in their lives.

If you are a person suffering from uneasiness or desolation or some other sort of psychosocial issue, get some mental fortitude, and find a trained therapist in cognitive behavior therapy. You can figure out how to make changes in your life and help yourself and the individuals around you. It might require some investment to see a difference in your life, yet to make sure you succeed in anything beneficial; you need assurance.

There are additionally numerous books which have been written regarding this matter you might need to look at. When going on the web, you can likewise find vast amounts of data that may assist you with learning much more about cognitive behavior therapy.

The time you may spend can make the difference. Fortunately, regardless of whether you feel overpowered and disheartened at times, there is help for you. There is additionally help in the type of classes you can to get familiar with cognitive behavior therapy and how it can help you. Setting aside some effort to investigate the data accessible might be your simple initial step to recuperation.

The Effectiveness of Cognitive Behavioral Therapy

Cognitive Behavioral Therapy (CBT) is a methodology that assists those with depression, and cognitive procedures dependent on a mix of essential behavioral and cognitive standards and strategies. CBT is problem-centered and activity situated methodology therapists use to enable patients to address specific problems, for example, nervousness, depression, and lots of increasingly complex mental issues.

Cognitive Behavioral Therapy alludes to several organized techniques for psychotherapy that get inside the musings behind a patient's issues. One overview of almost 2,300 analysts in the United States found that around 70 percent use CBT in combination with different treatments to treat depression and nervousness. CBT is additionally a prevalent psychotherapy worldview being taught in brain science advanced education programs.

How Cognitive Behavioral Therapy Works

Cognitive Behavioral Therapy depends on the possibility that people are to some degree, unreasonable and make a lot of strange mistakes whenever they survey the dangers and advantages of different circumstances and courses of their musings and activities. This can prompt wild feelings, for example, outrage and depression. Be that as it may, CBT is likewise used to treat an assortment of progressively complex issues, for instance, Post- Traumatic Stress Disorder (PTSD), OCD, substance abuse, ADHD, dietary issues, bipolar disorder, among different ailments.

Cognitive Behavioral Therapists must have decent compatibility with their patients for it to be compelling, for example, exceptional relational abilities and a suitable match in character types. This is because the patient and therapist cooperate in examining the current issues and the patient's intuition explanations for his or her musings and activities towards those issues. A definitive objective is to change figuring designs so the patient can encounter less incessantly negative enthusiastic states.

The National Alliance for Mental Health for CBT because it has excellent scientific information supporting its utilization in the clinical treatment of psychological maladjustment, and it has accomplished full prominence both for therapists and patients alike. A developing number of clinicians, therapists, social workers, and mental medical caretakers have training in CBT.

Research on the suitability of CBT is compelling for a broad scope of disorders. These investigations are well-controlled, the information is examined adequately, and the outcomes represent themselves. For instance, CBT has been found to give significant focal points in the treatment of bipolar disorder and bringing about fewer days in the emergency clinic, lower rates of suicide, and lower rates of para-self-destructive or self-harmful conduct.

Precautionary measures to Take Before Starting Cognitive Behavioral Therapy

Specialists, clinical analysts, social workers, and other emotional wellbeing experts finished long stretches of training and instruction. Nonetheless, it is conceivable to rehearse therapy without such a strong training foundation. A few things to explore before settling on a CBT specialist are instructive foundation and training, alongside any expert affiliations do they have a place with, for example, the Association for Behavioral and Cognitive Therapies, where most top therapists are individuals.

Before observing the creation of your first arrangement, check his or her experience, training, certification, and license. A psychotherapist is regularly utilized as a general term. Ensure that the therapist you pick meets state certification and authorizing requirements for his or her specific control. The key is to locate a talented therapist who can coordinate the type of therapy with your needs. Much of the time, CBT is best when it is joined with different treatments, for example, taking prescriptions. In this way, notwithstanding your therapist, you may likewise require a specialist for approving prescriptions.

Something else to consider is the expense. If you have medical coverage, discover what inclusion it offers for the therapy sessions. Some healthcare plans include just a specific number of therapy sessions a year. Some may not be secured by any means. Along these lines, make sure to converse with the therapist about charges and installment choices before your first visit.

Rundown

Before your first meeting, consider what problems you are having that need treatment. While you can likewise sort a portion of this out with your therapist, having a decent feeling of your issues ahead of time can help as a beginning stage. Once more, check for their qualifications and experience, specifically with your problems. Some therapists may not meet the requirements you need. If you don't locate the correct one the first run through, don't give up. Get your research done, and you will probably discover a decent Cognitive Behavioral Therapist.

Cognitive Behavioral Therapy - How Does This Method Work?

Cognitive-behavioral therapy is a talking strategy or a treatment for different sorts of problems, for example, eating and sleeping issues, nervousness problems, hurt feelings, tranquilizer abuse, behavior problems, personality issues and state of mind problems. CBT utilizes techniques and frameworks as a way to deal with different sorts of a social and obsessive issue.

There are a lot of methods used for this therapy, for example, rationalization behavior therapy, sound behavior therapy, as well as natural, emotive behavior therapy, cognitive therapy, and discerning living therapy. CBT is a two-route discussion, as the patient needs to express her contemplations and feelings while the specialist listens to, supports and mentors the patient.

The cognitive model of enthusiastic reaction that is cognitive behavioral therapy is an extraordinary one since its premise is that a person's musings are ground-breaking enough to change her behavior, feelings, and point of view. CBT is known as the sort of therapy that provides extraordinary outcomes in a shorter timeframe contrasted with different treatments and treatments.

CBT is additionally a period restricted therapy; anyway, it is likewise a ceaseless procedure. CBT gives a patient a chance to do tasks and take medications only when she is at home. The consequences of the undertaking or tasks are talked about and clarified during therapy sessions.

Beside ordinary therapy sessions, there are numerous valuable expert and self-improvement guides about cognitive behavioral therapy that will help a person who is encountering obsessive sadness. CBT has special techniques and recognition. Each session has a different program of the plan. Asking questions is significant in each CBT session. The patient needs to represent every one of her questions, and the specialists need to raise the patient-specific questions to have the option to address some of the things that the patient will be unable to express, as there are times when a patient will most likely be unable to determine what she truly feels.

Incredible methodologies are found out through Cognitive Behavioral Therapy, for example, having the option to change how people think and act. Thinking positive is likewise a part of CBT, which incorporates avoiding and putting a conclusion to programmed negative reasoning. The other productive procedures and techniques include deterring one's talking and strolling style. A patient additionally should be relaxed and comfortable, as it is simpler for the therapy to sink into a person's brain if he is comfortable and calm. The information provided to patients is likewise handled more naturally if a person isn't focused or forced.

Many reviews provide helpful information about cognitive behavioral therapy. Clarifications and models about CBT and the treatments are additionally posted. Circumstances and situations are submitted so family and companions of people with obsessive and social problems will have an idea of the problem and how to fix it. Any history of CBT and different examinations about it are accessible as well..

Let's explain better

Cognitive-behavioral therapy or CBT is a blend of two compelling treatments: cognitive and behavioral. Cognitive therapy applies to the thinking process and conviction framework, while behavioral therapy applies to individuals' activities. The structure of CBT was framed during the 1960s and is utilized in both individual and group therapy settings. It was created and refined by a few noticeable specialists, has gotten sufficient analysis from the phycological healthcare system and has stood the test of time and negativity.

While increasingly common treatments may take a very long time to help an individual experiencing a disorder, cognitive behavioral therapy is streamlined and takes as little as sixteen (16) sessions to see positive results. CBT is situated principally to client objectives and made to focus on and handle problems a client is encountering.

Cognitive-behavioral therapy has been found to be very compelling in anxiety disorders and phobia disorders such as schizophrenia; however, its range is extensive and deals with different sorts of diseases and dysfunctional behaviors. It mainly deals with the present time and place and to help accomplish the best results.

CBT's methodology is to attack the issue in earnest so as to talk and deal with problems head-on. It helps turn around negative thinking processes and changes practices through changing the thinking processes. It is found to be best if when a client finds the best thinking processes and activities for oneself, they then can execute them into their normal life.

For instance, cognitive-behavioral specialists may utilize techniques, for example,

> Instructing oneself to back off,

> Using positive attestations or fortifications to stop harmful and dangerous thinking,

> Give close consideration to voices one tunes into and voices that drive an individual to do certain things, and

> Concentrating consideration onto specific inspirations.

When thinking processes are resolved and being dealt with, behavioral therapy starts. It includes executing cognitive techniques to ordinary and genuine circumstances. It frequently involves client "homework" assignments in which the client envisions actual conditions and applies learned techniques to conquer whatever is causing problems. Other "homework" may incorporate rehearsing positive cognitive methods a few times every day. When the mind shifts from the negative to the positive, another technique is polished, and the cycle proceeds until negative thinking and practices end.

The greatest real advantage of cognitive behavioral therapy is that it calls for the client to act. The client plays a progressively active role in his or her therapy to treat manifestations and disorders.

Cognitive-behavioral therapy makes viable positive results and assists with an assortment of disorders.

HOW DOES CBT REALLY WORK?

Will cognitive behavioral therapy for anxiety be viable? Understanding the system behind this kind of therapy is a significant initial step in addressing this inquiry. CBT is ordinarily done for a specific timeframe and in light of any particular objective, is not at all like talk therapy or analysis, which could proceed for quite a long time. The aim is to modify thoughts that underlie undesirable behaviors.

Cognitive Behavioral Therapy is established on the aim that behaviors are reactions to our thoughts, instead of responses to outside occasions. Since ideas are discovered, we can separate and unlearn our negative thoughts. After we can build up a positive example of thinking, our negative responses will stop. Under the consideration of an expert therapist, cognitive behavioral therapy separates a significant problem into smaller, increasingly cognitive problems. This enables the patient and therapist to cooperate to determine these little issues. For instance:

Jim is a depressed person. He deals with an imaginary throbbing painfulness once a day. He visits his doctor as often as possible with new symptoms for which the doctor can discover no reason; by and by, Jim keeps on being sure that he has a life compromising problem. Jim puts a great deal of time in on the Web, looking at sites for more data about different symptoms and diseases.

Jim and his CBT therapist would experience a process of isolating and articulating his negative thoughts, and after that putting positive thoughts in their place. Jim and his therapist may think of this arrangement:

"A throbbing painfulness is all in my mind. I realize my body is solid and sound since it has been completely looked at by my doctor. Since I am certain of my great health, I am truly anticipating returning to active living. I will release my agonies since they are not in my body, yet rather are in my mind. Rather than basically returning home and going to sleep, I expect to delight in my recently discovered quality and essentialness by going on lively walk."

This delineates the process of supplanting negative with positive thoughts to modify behaviors, although it is an incredibly hopeful model. It is anything but difficult to see that cognitive behavioral therapy for anxiety has the potential to support sufferers. Working with a prepared therapist is essential to the achievement of a CBT approach.

People who experience the ill effects of anxiety frequently clutch onto their convictions with a great deal of confidence. Attempting new and progressively reliable perspectives is the thing that the prepared professional will persuade the patient to do. This kind of therapy would be very challenging were it not for that expert direction.

So, is there a self-assistance approach to do cognitive behavioral therapy for anxiety? Sensibly, no. In any case, close activities much like CBT is an approach that is basic with various self-assistance options. Such an approach incorporates:

- Identify negative thinking

- Recognize that the apparent danger is in your mind – is not genuine.

- Search for another approach to thinking that focuses on more beneficial behaviors.

As you are thinking about your self-assistance options, it will be helpful to comprehend the segments of cognitive-behavioral therapy. Cognitive-behavioral therapy for anxiety can be costly, so for this and numerous different reasons, a sufferer might need to choose a self-assistance option.

Search for opportunities that emphasis on the various problems (not options that dig into an individual's past) and for options that urge the sufferer to move gradually and thoughtfully toward more advantageous mental examples. Neither CBT nor comparable arrangements are quick fixes. Even though cognitive-behavioral therapy for anxiety requires some investment and exertion, it isn't as extensive a process as some of the other different types of therapy. With commitment and diligence, cognitive behavioral therapy for anxiety can and does work for some people.

Cognitive Behavioral Therapy - Addiction

Treatment

Cognitive-behavioral therapy addiction treatment is a psychotherapeutic approach (talking therapy) to substance addiction treatment and recuperation just as various other mental disorders. It is an efficient method that is objective situated and takes care of issues related to the insights, broken behaviors, and feelings that are generally what numerous addictions come from. Be that as it may, these disorders may form because someone gets dependent on liquor or medications.

How does CBT work?

You will rapidly find that cognitive behavior therapy is fundamentally used to treat an assortment of behavioral and excessive disorders, including:

> Addiction

> Uneasiness disorders and fits of anxiety

> Depression

> Different phobias

The least sophisticated approach to depict how cognitive behavioral therapy works is that it helps the dependent individual to comprehend those personal feelings and contemplations that impact their behavior adversely or emphatically. It helps the individual to concentrate on a quite specific issue and is a commonly present moment in length. During the addiction treatment and recuperation process, the individual figures out how to identify (and after that change) those dangerous and additionally exasperating idea designs that contrarily sway their behavior.

The rudiments of cognitive-behavioral therapy

The fundamental reason or rule that CBT depends on is that our personal feelings and contemplations play an essential, primary role in the manner by which we act either alone or out in the public arena. For instance, consider the individual who invests a great deal of energy contemplating plane disasters, for example, accidents or runway mishaps and so he maintains a strategic distance from air travel. The essential objective of CBT is that the individual can figure out how to assume responsibility for managing and deciphering certain parts of their condition, although they can't control them.

As of late, cognitive behavioral therapy addiction treatment has turned out to be very prevalent with psychological wellness professionals and other treatment masters. Also, because CBT is a temporary arrangement, it is impressively more moderate than other sorts of addiction treatment and recuperation treatments. It is experimentally upheld and has a demonstrated reputation of successfully helping individuals to defeat behavioral disorders and substance conditions.

Different approaches to CBT

Psychological wellness professionals usually utilize one of three different approaches to cognitive behavioral therapy, including:

> Cognitive therapy

> Multi-modular therapy

> Levelheaded emotive therapy

So as should be obvious, cognitive-behavioral treatments can turn out to be extremely perplexing relying upon the individual and the seriousness of their addiction or behavioral disorder.

COGNITIVE BEHAVIOR THERAPY FOR ADDICTION

Cognitive Behavior Therapy is a promising treatment for a full scope of addictions. While the therapy itself isn't a treatment for any addiction, it very well may be utilized as a component of a more significant effective program and will enable somebody to recuperate all the more rapidly.

Many people don't understand the fundamentals of Cognitive Behavior Therapy. The fundamental hypothesis of the therapy is that an individual has his or her feelings and behaviors dependent on their contemplations, and not by anything that they do. While many people may think this is insane, there is some coherent premise to it.

Everybody has a choice in what they believe, and when they feel it. At times, you are stuck in specific situations that you cannot escape from in any capacity whatsoever. Be that as it may, if you change your essential reasoning, you can change how you will respond and what you will do in these situations.

This can sound exceptionally confounding; be that as

it may, it is incredibly straightforward when put into the setting. For instance, when somebody who is addicted to liquor experiences Cognitive Behavior Therapy, they are instructed to perceive and avoid situations where they could access liquor. The addict is additionally educated about methodologies they can use to adapt, on the off chance that they can't make tracks in the opposite direction from the circumstance.

Addicts who are not prepared to concede they have an issue are a terrible candidate for Cognitive Behavior Therapy. Not exclusively will they be reluctant to take an interest, yet the preparation won't help them by any stretch of the imagination, as they won't utilize the skills to avoid their addiction.

For addicts who are prepared to proceed with the therapy, there are two steps in the program. The initial step is a functional analysis. While this may sound unnerving, it is only a session where a therapist and an addict chats about the addict about their emotions and feelings encompassing their addiction. This might be the "ah-ha" moment for the addict, where they realize what was pushing them into their addiction. This may take several sessions; in any case, it is significant that the full image of the addiction be acknowledged before the subsequent stage is embraced.

When the therapist and the addict have experienced the functional analysis, the following step of the therapy is to have a skills session. This session will help train the addict in what they have to know to avoid going backsliding. As the initial step of the therapy, this session will take numerous sequences. It might necessitate that the addict unlearns old propensities, and learns appropriate adapting skills. When the therapist enables the addict to adapt new solid adapting skills and systems, the addict should be able to continue with the therapy.

Cognitive Behavior Therapy is a quick and precise methodology for addicts of any addiction to enable themselves to remain calm. They talk about how they were previously, during, and after their addiction. The addicts likewise talk about what they felt like. Once everything has been spread out on the table, the addict learns new adapting skills with the assistance of a therapist. The whole therapy takes between ten to fifteen sessions; be that as it may, it is well justified, despite all the trouble.

Characteristics of Cognitive Behavioral Therapy

Cognitive-Behavioral Therapy is a type of psychotherapy that goes for restoring people with a passionate issue by concentrating on behavioral examples and point of view of the individuals. It is a general term that utilized different approaches like sound cognitive therapy, emotive therapy, ADHD therapy, dialectic behavior therapy and so forth. Cognitive-behavioral therapy has the accompanying qualities:

I. Based on the cognitive model of reactions related to feelings: CBT is based on changing the thoughts and feelings of people inside instead of relying upon the outside environment, similar to people, occasions, or conditions. This helps the individual to act and feel better regardless of whether the circumstance doesn't change around him.

II. It is rapid: Cognitive-behavioral therapy is viewed as probably the quickest type of treatments implied for treating the mental issue. The formal therapy is finished when both the client and the therapist are happy with the improvement appeared, and the client secures skills to deal with comparable issues in the future.

III. Building up a decent remedial connection alongside centered approach: A definite relationship between the therapist and the client is vital for appropriate treatment. The therapist who pursues the CBT approach centers around outfitting their client with self-counseling skills and henceforth the client figures out how to wind up autonomous. This can happen just when the sufferer is okay with his/her therapist.

IV. The endeavors are collaborative: CBT therapists try to find out about the feelings and thoughts of their client. They attempt to assist them with achieving their objectives in life. The role of a therapist is to tune in, learn and educate simultaneously while the part of the client is to express his/her worries, phobias honestly, and to demonstrate a will to ingest what he gains from the therapist.

V. CBT is an organized and order approach towards treatment: A specific plan is set for each session of CBT. The systems educated to the client are lined up with their objectives.

VI. CBT theory is based on a model of acceptance: The inductive strategy is received to urge people to recognize fantasies and presumptions from the real world and reasonable items of life. This helps the individual to acknowledge the genuine and dispose of the incredible negative thoughts which draw him down.

VII. Homework for clients: The clients are approached to actualize the skills and methods which are educated to them during the therapy sessions. Without rehearsing them, the client can't defeat his/her concern. Subsequently, homework turns into an individual piece of Cognitive behavioral therapy.

IN ANOTHER WAY

Intellectual Behavior Therapy, or CBT, is a type of psychotherapy that is viable for a wide assortment of problems in a person's life like sorrow, addictive behaviors, nervousness, relationship problems, poor eating, OCD, and bipolar issue. CBC works by changing individuals' thoughts and convictions (Cognitive) and their dealings (behavior).

CBT incorporates an assortment of methodologies that include Rational Emotive Behavior Therapy (REBT), Rational Living Therapy (RLT), Rational Behavior Therapy (RBT),), Cognitive Therapy (CT), Acceptance and Commitment Therapy (ACT), Dialectical Behavior Therapy (DBT), Mindfulness-Based Cognitive Therapy (MBCT), Cognitive Behavioral Analysis System of Psychotherapy (CBASP), Behavioral Activation (BA), Integrative Couple Therapy (ICT) and Functional Analytic Psychotherapy (FAP).

Notwithstanding this decent variety, most Cognitive

Behavior Therapies have the accompanying attributes:

I. CBT is based on this thought discernment reason for passionate and behavioral reactions.

Person's perspective makes their feelings and behaviors, not outside things like occasions, circumstances, and individuals. Therefore, if we can change our thoughts, subsequently our attitudes and behaviors will change.

II. CBT is Time-Limited.

A course might be from six to 20 sessions. It will depend on a few components like the type of problem, the highlights of the client, therapist's involvement, and so on be that as it may, as I would like to think the client's change thinking propensities is the most significant factor to end CBT sessions.

III. To learn adapting skills

CBT has more skills for taking care of our problem. Individuals don't learn a skill just by perusing and tuning in, learning, and being first. Any skill requires hard practice. Discovering great reasoning and proper managing problems is like learning a swimming skill and surfing. When a person learns them and doesn't fear the sea and waves and appreciates them.

IV. CBT is a cooperative, organized, and objective situated.

CBT is a cooperative exertion between the therapist and the client or gathering individuals. The role of the therapist is to tune in, watch, educate, and inspire, and the client's position is to discuss her or his problems, learn, and practice. Sessions have a structure, and each session has a specific agenda. A therapist helps the client in accomplishing chosen objectives.

V. Doing homework in CBT.

Homework is perceived as a crucial part of CBT. Learning CBT skills takes quite a while. Homework is arranged by the type of problem and the client's prospects.

VI. Separately or group session

CHAPTER THREE
CBT- THE CURRENT TREATMENT OF CHOICE

Cognitive-behavioral therapy is as of now getting a significant level of consideration as the treatment of choice for people requiring help with an assortment of mental issues. It is an organized, practical way to deal with managing problems and is speaking to those looking for treatment. Individuals needing guidance are searching out clinicians who have particular training in CBT. Understanding the purpose behind this present pattern in the reputation of cognitive-behavioral therapy can be found in the one of a kind qualities which are critical to this methodology of treatment. There is a straightforwardness but then competence in the model which describes the ideas of CBT.

Cognitive-behavioral therapy encourages a community connection between the patient and therapist. Together, the patient and counselor build up confidence in a relationship and commonly talk about the revealing problems to be organized and investigated in therapy. In CBT, the top issue that needs to be addressed, disturbing the patient usually turns into the underlying focal point of treatment. Subsequently, the patient will, in general, feel eased and eager that the essential problem that brought him to therapy is promptly being recognized and tended to.

Problems are handled head-on in a down to earth way. The patient is trained on the ABC's of cognitive-behavioral therapy. The therapist clarifies the association among thoughts and convictions and their effect on conduct. How the patient sees problems decides the way wherein the individual reacts to different issues. It's the way of thinking about life's questions that steer the patient's way of acting.

How about we accept that you work in an office and for a whole week an associate has strolled past you without recognizing your value. Every day you return to your workspace and wonder why this coworker is mistreating you. You develop thoughts about her being condescending and pretentious and start addressing what you may do to interrupt her.

Outrage starts to rise, and you begin thinking, "How could she treat me along these lines!" Eventually, you settle down and start to think about the problem judiciously. You think, "This is dumb, why don't I go visit her at her office and see what's happening in her life that may influence this circumstance. You enter her office and start a discussion.

Amidst your talk, she uncovers her child is experiencing unhappiness and needs to see a counselor. Your associate is frustrated about the circumstance and confides in you that she has been tense with everybody at the office. She inquires as to whether you are aware of a qualified therapist. You give her a few thoughts, and before you leave, she gets up from her seat and gives you a firm embrace. This occurrence exhibits how our thinking can be broken and can be founded on some wrong assumptions.

CBT is viable in the light of the fact it instructs the patient to modify examples of thinking which influence conduct. CBT is a straight-forward therapy which is intended to caution the patient about pointless ways of thinking. Finding twisted or maladaptive thinking is practiced through an exploratory process which is dependent upon a reliable patient/counselor effective partnership.

Cognitive-behavioral therapy centers around the patient's negative self-talk and offers reasonable recommendations on the most proficient method to untwist one's thinking to make it increasingly versatile. The CBT therapist helps the client in thinking all the more generally by looking at the person's spontaneous thoughts, watching ways in which they may mutilate reality, and uncovering underlying assumptions or convictions that influence their ways of thinking and acting.

Spontaneous thoughts are simply the nonsensical things we say when we are under pressure - "I'll never get a date, who would ever need me!" Cognitive contortions are the focal points from which we see reality - "You always make me feel like a washout" (either-or thinking). Underlying assumptions are the "hot catches" which take shape as a way of adapting and getting our needs met during adolescence - "I should maintain a strategic distance from strife no matter what; I hate objection and getting my feelings hurt."

Cognitive-behavioral therapy looks to discredit the nonsensical things we let ourselves know and helps us in growing increasingly objective ways of responding to our maladaptive points of view. Since homework is a vital piece of therapy, patients will be urged to finish activities intended to change negative thinking. One reliable technique encourages the client to identify current alarming occasions, negative self-talk, and ways of objectively responding to circumstances sited. The individual logs difficult situations that define pointless thinking and discredit the negative ways of thinking with all the more deeply, versatile ways of responding to events. During every therapy session, the log sheet is checked on for patient advancement.

With CBT, clients are responsible for their very own advancement. They know about the process that is important for change, and perseveringly work at modifying flawed idea strategies. The therapeutic progress is effectively checked through self-inventories and patient criticism. Time is always left toward the finish of sessions to audit the advantages or entanglements of the directing sessions. Clients are asked to evaluate the appropriateness they get from their counselor's treatment process.

Patients frequently ask, "how much time will this guiding treatment take?" Although each case is unique, six to eight sessions are commonly adequate to show clients methodologies for reshaping their thinking. CBT is a period restricted, easy to use, practical process for helping people to survey their negative thinking and cause a necessary change in the way they to react to themselves, as well as to other people.

People with tension, addictive examples, and complicated issues are especially appropriate to profiting from this form of treatment. Fortunately, numerous social wellbeing issues can be dealt with effectively through cognitive-behavioral therapy. NACBT or The National Association of Cognitive-Behavioral Therapy is a decent asset for finding counselors who are adequately prepared, certified, and have some expertise in this treatment approach.

CBT - Cure Your Anxiety Condition!

There is a permanent cure for the broad scope of anxiety conditions, including frenzy disorder, over the top urgent disorder, post-traumatic stress disorder, summed up as anxiety disorder, social anxiety disorder, and phobias. As indicated by the National Institute For Mental Health (NIMH), anxiety disorders plague 40 million American adults ages 18 and up. As we think about the significance of that fantastic number, how about we examine the prescribed strategy for treatment, one that has provided improvement to countless sufferers.

Cognitive-behavioral therapy is a converging of two particular treatments, the two of which follow their foundations back to the 1950s and 1960s- - and their acknowledgment by the medical establishment in the 1970s and 1980s.

Cognitive therapy was created during the 1960s by American specialist Aaron T. Beck. Beck initially linked his way of dealing with issues of depression, and at that point, extended his training to incorporate anxiety disorders. How individuals translate their everyday lives, and relegate importance is a procedure called insight. Beck, disappointed with customary psychotherapeutic diving into the intuitive, reasoned that cognizance, what his patients saw, was the way to powerful therapy that would prompt dependable recovery.

When building up his therapy, Beck previously seen that discouraged individuals embrace a negative perception of the world during their developmental years-- in light of the departure of a friend or family member, peer dismissal, analysis by power figures, discouraged attitudes present in significant others, in addition to a large group of arbitrary negative occasions.

Frequently, this negative perception is nourished and supported by a one-sided, passionate perspective on the world- - for instance, win or lose deduction, over-speculation, and specific perceptions that prohibit crucial significant data. Cognitive therapy postulates that contortions in a person's points of view develop into disorders. It is the job of a cognitive therapist to call attention to these mutilations and boost change in a sufferer's attitude.

Behavior therapy made its presentation in 1953, in the United States, in an examination undertaking headed by B.F. Skinner. In South Africa, Joseph Wolpe and his exploration gathering are credited with spearheading work. In the United Kingdom, Hans Eysenck added to the advancement of this sort of therapy.

Behavior therapy depends principally on the practical investigation. Behavioral therapists have effectively been utilized as a treatment for intimacy issues, endless agony, stress, anorexia, constant distress, substance abuse, clinical depression, and anxiety.

Behavior therapy is information-driven and logical, focusing on the earth and its specific situation. Behavior therapy is concerned about the impact or outcome of Behavior. Behavior is seen as factually unsurprising, A person is treated on the whole, without the diversions of a psyche versus body approach, however, connections, 2-way relationships, are very much considered.

Initially, anxiety conditions were seen as side-effects of synthetic lopsided characteristics or possibly hereditary inclinations. As these thoughts were abandoned, learned behaviors were credited as the source of most anxiety conditions. Trust in a permanent cure developed, and, during the 1990s, cognitive therapy and behavioral therapy converged into cognitive behavioral therapy (CBT). The shared opinion for these two treatments is accentuation on the "here and now" by concentrating on reducing indications and supplanting hurtful, foolish Behavior with helpful convictions and attitudes.

In the United Kingdom, the National Institute for Health and Clinical Excellence suggests CBT as favored treatment for emotional well-being difficulties, for example, OCD, post-traumatic stress disorder, bulimia, clinical depression, and notwithstanding for the neurological condition endless weakness disorder. In the United States, notwithstanding our fixation on pharmaceutical arrangements, CBT became known inside the medical establishment. Gifted, results-driven assistance is accessible for sufferers who look for it.

There you have it. The ugly truth is out in the open. Doctor prescribed prescriptions? Not required. A permanent cure for anxiety conditions? Inside your grasp!

If you experience the ill effects of anxiety in any of its horrific manifestations, genuinely the best and most qualified person that you know is holding on for you to look for expert help by way of an authorized cognitive-behavioral therapist. That person, consistently on your side, continuously to the rescue when you need it most, is you!

Cognitive Behavioral Therapy and Overcoming Stress

For those searching for methods of overcoming anxiety, there are various choices accessible that can be considered "regular." What do those usual anxiety relief methods include? These are hostile to anxiety procedures that don't include the utilization of solution pills or medications as a means of lightening the problem. Regularly, these methods prove to be far healthier than what the abused methods of treating anxiety convey. One such process of overcoming anxiety is cognitive-behavioral therapy.

Cognitive-behavioral therapy isn't something new. Mental health professionals have employed it for quite a long time as a means of changing the conduct decisions an individual makes that makes up mental health issues. Cognitive-behavioral therapy is not exclusively been utilized as a method for defeating uneasiness, it has even been utilized to treat other profoundly genuine mental health issues too. All in all, what does cognitive therapy involve? Here is a short diagram of what it entails:

As a type of anxiety relief; the cognitive behavioral therapy includes adopting a two-dimensional strategy to fix the problem. This first half involves managing the cognitive issues which causes the anxiety. That is, the musings and mental segments of the problem will be examined. The psychological triggers that cause stress will be considered, and after that means produced to turn around the trigger results will be established.

The behavioral therapy segment for overcoming anxiety is the opposite side of the coin. This methodology manages the real triggers identified with physical activities or activities that can cause a concern-based response. Likewise, with the mental segment to cognitive therapy, the objective with behavioral therapy is to modify one's trigger response to activities that achieve anxiety.

Some may have genuine worries regarding whether this kind of therapy can prompt discernible outcomes as far as overcoming anxiety. Honestly, there is nothing to be worried about because cognitive-behavioral therapy has been demonstrated to be a viable treatment method for quite some time. This is, without a doubt, not another treatment methodology as it has been employed by therapists and other mental health professionals for incredible accomplishment for a long time.

One of the primary reasons why cognitive behavioral therapy fills in as a means of improving one's ability to increase genuinely necessary anxiety relief fixates on the way that a great many people are ignorant of what causes their anxiety. In a stunning number of examples, the triggers that cause the beginning of anxiety, stress, or a fit of anxiety are obscure to the individual encountering the problem. Through working with an advisor, the ability to get to the core of what is making the stress ends up conceivable. From this, overcoming anxiety ends up conceivable because the foundation of the problem is identified.

Overcoming anxiety without getting to the core of decreasing stress in your life is a practically inconceivable undertaking. If you need to experience anxiety relief, usually, you should assume responsibility for everything in your life that is causing you stress and anxiety.

CHAPTER FOUR
COGNITIVE BEHAVIORAL THERAPY AND MEDICATIONS

If you have an anxiety disorder, a fundamental inquiry that you may pose to yourself is: "How can I improve?" If you happen to bring this up to your primary care physician, they are in all respects liable to recommend you a drug without referencing the best, scientifically approved treatment around: Cognitive Behavioral Therapy or CBT for short. In the course of the last 20 or 30 years or somewhere in the vicinity, researchers have found a few rules that help people conquer their phobias. These standards have to do with how thinking influences or colors enthusiastic reactions and how specific practices contribute either to supportive and versatile passionate responses or excruciating and difficult ones. These standards added to the arrangement of another kind of therapy called Cognitive-Behavioral Therapy.

The Cognitive part (which means thinking) works by teaching people to change hurtful, excessively fearful, and non-sensible edgy thinking into progressively constructive and reasonable perspectives. The fundamental supposition that is: If you change how you think, you will change the way you feel. The Behavioral part works by teaching people to take part in practices that have a quieting impact on decreasing edgy excitement,

54

and by adopting new conduct to confront, instead of maintaining a strategic distance from phobias through a procedure of Therapeutic Exposure to the concern. Intellectual Behavioral approaches for Anxiety Disorders are better than medication in decreasing anxiety and forestalling failure. Still, most Americans have once in a while known about it, and since numerous therapeutic specialists don't have prepared access to this approach, medication is frequently endorsed for anxiety disorders.

Let's investigate the significant classes of drugs used to "treat" anxiety disorders. There are two primary classes of medication most generally recommended to treat anxiety: Tranquilizers (a level or gathering of Benzodiazepine based meds like Xanax, Ativan, and Valium) and antidepressants (like Paxil, Prozac, Wellbutrin, and Zoloft). There are many, a lot more too. The latest research recommends that while Benzodiazepine medications work quicker, there are numerous problems related to their utilization (anxiety bounce and including withdrawal when they are ceased). The ugly truth is that drugs are likewise connected with an assortment of disagreeable symptoms: weight gain, sexual problems (like difficulty in getting an erection and climax), dry mouth, migraines, gastrointestinal trouble, and numerous others.

Another significant problem with all classes of drug treatment for anxiety disorders is that once the drug is stopped, the odds of a relapse are a lot more prominent than after a practical course of Cognitive Behavioral Therapy. The essential truth is that drugs work while you take them! If you learn specific adapting abilities through CBT, they become a piece of you for the remainder of your life, bringing about significantly diminished anxiety even after treatment has finished.

Psychological Behavioral approaches to passionate problems have been indicated over and again by thorough scientific examinations to significantly diminish alarm, anxiety, stress, and fear in an assortment of all-around controlled investigations. It has now been shown that for certain Anxiety Disorders (Agoraphobia and including Panic Disorder), that these approaches have better results and far less relapse then medication (again, when you go off the drug, the manifestations sooner or later for the most part return).

A great many people are uninformed of these discoveries since the medication is by a long shot still the most widely recognized treatment for anxiety problems. Lamentably, per above, medication does not instruct abilities! Mind imaging studies have demonstrated that after people experienced a course of Cognitive Behavioral Therapy, they encountered a lessening in the fear motivation of the brain!

Cognitive Behavioral Therapy for Treating Autism

A couple of behavioral medications have been tried from time to time for treating children with autism. Necessary response getting ready and associated direct assessment are two of the most promoted. Regardless, adults, older children, and teenagers are most likely going to benefit more from cognitive behavioral therapy, another genuine intervention to treat autism.

There have been various undertakings to change cognitive behavioral therapy for teenagers and older children having autism. The target has generally been on the individuals who experience the evil impacts of anxiety. Additionally, in light of the way, this is a distinctive trademark in autism. Challenges have been to check regardless of whether mentally unbalanced youngsters have aptitudes that are required for psychological social treatment to be a success.

The response, fortunately, is in the proof. An ongoing report surveyed the cognitive abilities of older children with autism and differentiated them and those of non-autistic children. Each tyke in the previous gathering had subjective conduct abilities and they could perceive angles, practices, and thoughts. They found it challenging to see feelings.

Conventional cognitive behavioral therapy calls for demanding discourse and dynamic thinking limits, and this is regularly a challenge for those having autism. Researchers have understood this and have modified the therapy to suit autistic individuals, for example, making it even more ostensibly captivating and concrete, and repetitive. For instance, just asking the kids to verbally rank their nervousness on a size of one to 10, a specialist may have a thermometer that exhibits the uneasiness level from low to high, and approach the individuals to demonstrate the prop for outlining this.

Another framework in cognitive behavioral therapy for autism incorporates focusing on a child's capacity and exceptional interests that help to keep the children stimulated and involved, and manufacture visit material activities and improvement breaks for the individuals who may have assumed deficiency issues with under or over-reactivity.

The researchers saw that direct cognitive therapy must address social skills among those with autism since focus social shortages among energetic individuals with autism add to anxiety which by then continues to intensify the teens social issues.

The therapy can be passed on in a couple of different ways, like family, individual, groups, and even the two families and groups. Group remedies have a bit of breathing space that an individual with autism can see near different individuals engaging with comparable difficulties and endeavoring to blend them together. Social assistance and friendship expanded through the methodology could be patching in themselves.

A family behavioral therapy for autism as often as possible incorporates guardians who teach themselves about their children's challenges. It moreover includes teaching them to invigorate using cognitive behavioral therapy techniques when an authentic condition is facing the child. This will make them feel sure and happy for contributing a positive change in a child's life.

Researchers have found that the issue of protecting

children from a possibly negative experience, is regularly an outrageous call for the majority of guardians. Autistic children, when in doubt, have a foundation set apart by behavioral and eager challenges and of anguishing veritable dissatisfactions on the planet. Their folks are sometimes reluctant to approach the child to encourage frustrations, and inadvertently limit the introduction to experiences imperative to end up being not as anxious yet somewhat increasingly independent.

Obsessive-Compulsive Disorder Cognitive Behavioral Therapy

When a patient is determined to have OCD or obsessive compulsive disorder, the run of the mill form of treatment includes a blend of antidepressant medications and mental therapy. While there are numerous forms of psychiatric therapy, the one that has been discovered the best for the treatment of OCD is "CBT" or "cognitive behavior therapy."

Cognitive behavior therapy is focused upon the hypothesis that our thoughts or observations control the way we respond or act and not our condition, situations, or circumstances. In this way, by changing the way we want and likewise to change how we react to these situations.

CBT - Response and Exposure Prevention

The introduction and response prevention method used in individual conduct therapy is utilized to enable the patient to get control over their compulsions by presenting them their fixations and afterward having them abstain from completing their impulsive conduct.

For example, if an individual has the compulsion of washing their hands too much, they will be approached to shake hands for instance, shown a doorknob and afterward stopped from washing their hands. This method has been demonstrated to be convincing as the urgent desire will, in general leave after a moderately brief timeframe all by itself.

After temporarily using this method of desensitization, the patient starts to understand that they never again need to follow-up on their compulsions to ease their anxiety. This kind of intellectual conduct therapy has been influential in decreasing and notwithstanding taking out a portion of the addictions in patients with OCD. By confronting their feelings of dread, the patient likewise figures out how to deal with their undesirable thoughts or fixations to soothe their anxiety.

Psychological Therapy for OCD

The psychological therapy used for patients with obsessive compulsive disorder centers around the burning thoughts that cause the person to take part in their habitual conduct. The irrational or nonsensical ideas are tested by having the patient gauge the rates or the probability that their feelings of dread could turn into a reality.

When the patient has figured out how to perceive their nonsensical thoughts, they are shown the abilities to supplant them with progressively sound and positive thoughts and furthermore, methods of relaxing schemes that can be utilized to quiet themselves in specific situations that have recently set off their anxiety.

By and large, patients with excessive compulsive disorder will start to see an improvement after just a couple of sessions of individual social therapy. Notwithstanding, if you suffer from OCD you will need to guarantee that you get an advisor who spends significant time in this sort of therapy for the treatment of anxiety disorders as not all specialists are prepared or qualified in individual social therapy.

It has been discovered that it isn't extraordinary for some people who have OCD to get long stretches of therapy that is lacking to treat their condition and that has been known to worsen the side effects in certain people with OCD.

How to Tell If Your Therapist Uses Cognitive Behavioral Therapy

Much of the time posed inquiries that I got, as all certified cognitive therapist and supporter of Cognitive Behavioral Therapy (CBT), is how you should say why a therapist uses CBT. To be completely forthright, I likewise discover this qualification to be difficult, since such huge numbers of therapists guarantee that they use this type of therapy in their practice.

I once in a while, meet a therapist who doesn't state they practice CBT. While I am not inferring that therapists lie about what they do, frequently they have been presented to a modest quantity of CBT and are not adequately trained.

Superficially, cognitive behavioral therapy is moderately necessary, as it's permanently changing your thoughts and behavior to feel better inwardly, however, as a general rule, it takes a great deal to be fully trained in how to use this with clients adequately. Although there is no foolproof approach to tell whether your therapist is utilizing CBT with you, there are a few qualities to look for that will make you an educated shopper.

CBT Characteristic #1: Addresses Your Thoughts and Behaviors

A genuine CBT therapist will spend quite a bit of your session investigating the behaviors, thoughts, and feelings that are associated with your fundamental concerns. Frequently they will use what's known as a thought record or, as David Burns, writer of the top-rated self-improvement guide *Feeling Good*, calls it, an "Everyday Mood Log" to enable you to catch and afterward take a shot at your negative thoughts.

Practically all therapists will examine your feelings, in any event, I trust along these lines, yet what sets CBT therapists apart is their extra attention on your thoughts and behaviors. As opposed to accepting every one of your troubles originates from early youth problems or a horrible past, CBT therapists will look to your ideas to figure out what to do straight away. Regularly your thoughts and behaviors will be programmed or to some degree covered up in nature, and attempting to coax them out and address them gives substantial help and significant life enhancements.

CBT Characteristic #2: Focused and Agenda Driven

Numerous therapists who don't use CBT regularly will offer guidance and be commonly healthy. However, this can prompt a perpetual survey of your emotions and restrict progress. Cognitive-behavioral therapists, albeit intense and outfitted towards your interests too, differ in that they will set an agenda every session to make sure progress is being made or possibly set some structure to make however much progress as could reasonably be expected with every session.

This generally includes a short recap of the week, audit of the homework that was appointed and territories that still should be tended to, time for practicing schemes, and criticism about the therapy. Albeit every single good therapist will be adaptable somewhat depending upon what's going on for you at the time, an excessive amount of adaptability, joined with the absence of an agenda, regularly prompts baffling outcomes.

CBT Characteristic #3: Tracks Your Symptoms

CBT therapists more often than not screen your manifestations or the problems that carried you to guiding, in some composed way. As opposed to merely asking you how you are feeling, they will in general use state-administered tests or scales to look out for the problems that you are searching for assistance with. By utilizing such devices, CBT therapists can spot patterns and rapidly respond by adjusting their therapy to suit your immediate needs. This regular checking likewise permits the therapist and the client both to look at how guiding is proceeding to make choices about how to continue.

CBT Characteristic #4: Gives You Helpful Homework

Homework is a sign of CBT therapists - and any good therapists, as I would like to think. The exploration is evident that if you do homework as a significant aspect of your therapy, you will show signs of improvement quicker and make more progress during your time in advising.

Homework is a prerequisite of cognitive-behavioral therapy since such an extensive amount of the guiding is tied in with learning and rehearsing new abilities. Envision how much more you can do in the week outside of the 50 minutes that you go through with your therapist, and when your accomplished therapist guides that work, the outcomes are even more dominant.

This being stated, not all homework is made equivalent, and an accomplished CBT therapist will most likely clarify why specific homework is advantageous or required.

CBT Characteristic #5: Has Received Certification

One optimistic, yet later, approach to decide whether your therapist has some strong CBT aptitudes is to check whether the individual in question is certified by the Academy of Cognitive Therapy (academyofct.org). This is an association created for merely this reason: to show clinical competence in cognitive therapy for clients looking for treatment. Getting to be certified requires a great deal of preparation in CBT, letters of recommendation from associates, and a broad depiction of how you use CBT in your practice, including a sound tape of an authenticated client session (don't stress, the client must give authorization).

Looking for therapy is an excellent method to improve your sentiments of tension, sorrow, and stress, and realizing who to see makes it all the more straightforward. If you're searching for tried and true and powerful treatment, for example, cognitive behavioral therapy, the rundown above can set you up in the correct way and help you locate a qualified therapist to help you improve your life.

CHAPTER FIVE
CHANGE YOUR PROBLEM BEHAVIORS, CHANGE YOUR LIFE!

Insomnia is a condition which perpetrates millions consistently causing worldwide pressure and misery. Regularly, these sleep disturbing influences comprise of either having a difficult time getting the chance to rest or awakening frequently for the duration of the night. There are various cures accessible available today that when done without hesitation, are expected to halt this muddled issue, yet a significant number of them have been demonstrated not to succeed. Many insomniacs search out common cures for lack of sleep. One such mainstream regular cure is known as cognitive behavior therapy. Let's examine this in more detail.

When a person can't sleep, it might be the consequence of different torments. Many experience this sort of sleep disturbing influence since they are experiencing large amounts of worry in their consistent life. Insomnia can likewise happen as a symptom of over-the-counter and prescription drugs. Various ailments can prompt sleeplessness, for example, Fibromyalgia. The taking of recreational drugs, and drinking a lot of liquor may likewise bring about lack of sleep issues.

Numerous characteristic natural cures exist that are

accessible to people who suffer with insomnia. Probably the most regularly known about these normal cures incorporates the utilization of Melatonin and Valerian Root. Different ways are marked "characteristic" when it comes to beating insomnia. One of the most widely recognized reasonable solutions for insomnia that isn't homegrown is the utilization of cognitive behavior therapy.

Psychological Behavior Therapy, or CBT, is one of the best and most up to date methods for relieving the discouraging issue of insomnia. Numerous individuals are quick to attempt this therapy as it is the most secure option in contrast to prescription medications or drugs. It has been built up that sufferers who have severe insomnia cases have regularly taken prescription medications for an exceptionally significant sum of time. In any case, one of the incredible advantages of CBT is that people who are interested keep an eye on needing it on a brief premise to cure their absence of sleep.

Psychological behavior therapy works around the premise that you are absolutely what you think you are. You take the activities precisely as you might suspect you should take them. The psyche is the one single power that will be adjusted before some other changes can happen. An official capable figure must perform this sort of therapy to cure your insomnia naturally. This expert will attempt a set amount of sessions to change the entire way of thinking of the person suffering with insomnia.

To begin with, the expert will work with the person who can't sleep properly to make a customized arrangement geared towards the person. Initially, the person will be educated on the base amount concerning sleep being essential to stay stable. Numerous thoughts and hypotheses will be examined during an initial couple of training sessions.

From here, an individual will be required to take part in training activities and meetings. These training sessions are genuinely low exertion and don't involve any requirement for physical perseverance. Or maybe, they will include a "psychological reconstructing session" of what the person thinks about sleep.

All through the span of these reinventing sessions, the individual will be educated regarding the activities they are required to perform with the goal that they can generally cure their insomnia. The behaviors they get may comprise of awakening at precisely the same time each morning, and hitting the sack simultaneously consistently - this is all part of the reprogramming. Besides, the individual may likewise be advised to get a set amount of sunlight always, take out naps, and notwithstanding working in occasional spells of physical exercise.

Specialists accept that utilizing cognitive behavior therapy to cure the issues related to insomnia usually is amazingly profitable and productive. When a person has embraced a set amount of sessions, their contemplations are expected to change, so that cures insomnia typically. If you or somebody that you know is experiencing the discouraging condition of sleepless nights, specialists concur that cognitive behavior therapy might be your best and top option in contrast to prescription drugs.

Weight Management Using Cognitive-Behavioral Therapy

Diets bomb time after time. People set grandiose exercise objectives with no finish since it's simpler not to do it. There are such a significant number of things that turn out badly with a conventional diet and exercise program that it's no big surprise that more people are searching for better approaches to lose weight and get healthy for the last time.

Clinicians have perceived continuously the need to change the whole person versus customary diets and exercise routines. Intellectual Behavioral Therapy (CBT) is one way that advisors are attempting to make a change from the back to front with people who need to lose lots of weight and find a healthy lifestyle.

The mind-body connection to weight management is a lot more grounded than numerous people understand. Dieting and exercise go the extent that a person's mind will permit. Somebody who needs ambition and completion won't see as much accomplishment from a weight loss program as somebody who is led to succeed. The utilization of Cognitive-Behavioral Therapy attempts to change the reasoning first, and afterward, the physical appearance will turn because the mindset has been adjusted. By basically re-programming and retraining the mind-body connection, advisors can help people lose weight, get healthy, and keep up that healthy lifestyle on into the future.

Yo-yo diets are a prime case of what happens when you attempt to change the body without the mind being part of the change. People regularly do very well for a brief span when they choose to change what they eat. In the long run, nonetheless, their old propensities grab hold and the weight returns because their mindset has not been altered by any means.

It has been demonstrated that people who prevail at weight management are the individuals who experience treatment or some guiding simultaneously to get their mind into the perfect spot while likewise taking a shot at their body. When diets, exercise, meds, or even medical procedures aren't sufficient to keep people hale and healthy, CBT can add that additional push to help give people the healthy lifestyle that they have frequently desired.

Having an immediate association with a specialist can make a reliable mind-body connection to weight management and help people to deliver better outcomes since they have an individual arrangement. Through things like CBT, contemplation, and self-observing, people can figure out how to change how they think, which at that point enables them to change how they eat, exercise, and live their lives.

The objective is the equivalent no matter how you look at it: making a healthy lifestyle and changing an entire person, so the wellbeing is both physical and mental, as opposed to concentrating on the physical without anyone else's input.

The reason that diets regularly don't work and that

exercise routines are always 'wishful thinking,' and little else is because the propensities and mindset of the people attempting to lose weight are unchanged. Until the whole person is tended to and an entirely different healthy lifestyle for mind and body is made, weight loss might be fleeting, best case scenario.

Cognitive Behavior Therapy For Back Pain

Cognitive behavior therapy (CBT), as the name recommends, goes for changing the disposition or the thinking designs of the individual. The articulation is to develop positive thinking and get rid of a negative rationale. How you judge the circumstances decides how you respond to it. It depends on the confidence in the strength of your thinking or as the expression goes: the mind can move mountains.

Cognitive therapy helps the general population to identify the contortions in their reasoning (perception). If you imagine that a glass is half unfilled, you tend to feel terrible, and if you believe that it is half full, you tend to feel better. Cognitive behavior therapy attempts to advance the high vibe factor by helping you to discover motivations to explore cheerfully.

This therapy stresses the positive reaction to back pain to cope with it. If you have a long history of severe pain, you tend to freeze at the scarcest trace of pain or distress whatsoever. The dread of pain itself triggers physical changes, for example, stiffening of the muscles and a raise in blood pressure. As the muscles become tense, they cause even more pain.

An expectation of joy, then again, triggers sound mental and physiological changes in the mind and body. It improves the blood circulation, which flushes out the inflammatory components from the body. It likewise acquires more oxygen that empowers the blood vessels.

In all actuality, cognitive behavioral therapy does not intend to fix the back pain, yet it helps the patient by showing him how to manage it. It is apparent that over thinking assumes an urgent role by the way we respond to the pain. In a down to earth sense, cognitive behavior therapy shows you relaxation techniques that diminish the strain in the muscles by occupying the thoughts from thinking about the pain.

Restrictions of cognitive behavior therapy

There is no uncertainty that our idea examples do enable us to cope with the pain; it is likewise a reality that the truth of pain can't be disregarded. If you have seriously harmed your muscle from a high fall, you can't merely wish away the severe pain. Cognitive behavior therapy can't get rid of the reason for the pain. You need to take medications to dispose of it. It, obviously helps, during the time spent recuperating from pain.

Using Cognitive Behavior Therapy (CBT) For Panic Attacks

If you need to look for a treatment that includes talking and guiding, Cognitive Behavioral Therapy (CBT) has been observed to be an effective course for around half of the individuals who experience the ill effects of panic attacks or agoraphobia. Cognitive Behavioral Therapy plans to change your thoughts and behavior and is measurably demonstrated to have a high achievement rate when treating anxiety, panic attacks, and phobias.

Cognitive Behavioral Therapy works since it endeavors to both help you process why you might have the thoughts you have, thus paving the way to a panic attack and after that help, you change your behaviors to enable you to oversee them with your situation examining one method. CBT is made of two components, cognitive therapy, and behavior therapy.

Cognitive therapy depends on the possibility of the way we think triggers panic attacks. Any destructive or unbeneficial thinking examples are worked through and identified alongside deceptions or thoughts you may have. This will show the sufferer how to see their thought patterns, and see how they are misjudging occasions and making programmed negative thoughts winding wild, thus bringing about anxiety and panic attacks.

Behavior Therapy focuses on how you respond to things which trigger anxiety, or sentiments you connect with the beginning of anxiety. The advisor will assist you with walking through those situations that trigger an attack and help you feel progressively sure and in charge, decreasing the commonness' of a panic attack in these circumstances. This may incorporate the utilization of mantras or breathing methods.

CBT is broadly used to fix the anxiety issue, and this is a strategy to re-program your mind's response to the trigger of anxiety attacks. In any case, it won't be figured out in a couple of sessions, mainly if the panic issue is an entrenched piece of your regular day to day existence.

Cognitive Behavioral therapy is the most prescribed treatment for controlling panic attacks. The rule lies on the presumption that the individual's state of mind depends on just examples of feelings. CBT centers around negative feeling acknowledgment, evaluation of its legitimacy, and substitution of unconstructive responses into something more beneficial and progressively fitting for the body.

Definition

CBT is different from other treatments for the accompanying reasons:

I.   The therapy focuses on two specific tasks - the immediate present and cognitive rebuilding. It changes how an individual reacts to stressors, and it enables an individual to conquer impediments.

II.   CBT organizes objectives.

III.   An instructive methodology is followed in the

program. Patients are approached to record their reaction to worry, just like the coping strategies they use.

IV.   Patients keep up a functioning job in CBT. They identify their negative musings and find ways to control them.

V.   The program incorporates a few strategies: behavioral analyses, guided disclosure, symbolism, pretending, and Socratic addressing.

VI.   The treatment procedure is constrained and will keep going for just 3 to 4 months.

Target Group

Cognitive Behavioral therapy is foremost in controlling panic attacks for these accompanying groups or conditions:

- Individuals are encountering calm to a direct instance of panic tension.

- Patients who don't wish to take a prescription.

- The pre-adult age group who has encountered continuous failures.

- Adults who have not reacted well to other treatment options.

- Anyone who is driven and who can control and train one's self.

The Standard Procedure

CBT is rendered by emotional wellness experts who have gotten special training to direct the therapy. The procedure may differ starting with one wellbeing expert then onto the next, yet the sessions regularly have the accompanying layout:

> The patient is checked for manifestations of a panic attack.

> The advisor sets a calendar for meetings.

> Assignments are given to the patient and followed up during the next meeting.

> Problems are talked about, and coping strategies will be taught for controlling panic attacks.

> The session closes with an evaluation from the advisor and criticism from the two meetings.

> Usually, one session would keep going for 50 minutes to 60 minutes.

Cognitive Behavioral therapy enables the individual to decide the issue and find ways to beat it. A definitive objective is to find methods that are proficient and helpful in controlling panic attacks. For other treatment options, visit our site and find the best solution for nervousness.

ANSWER TO PANIC ATTACKS

People who experience the ill effects of panic attacks experience symptoms, for example, heart palpitations, sweating, loss of control, feelings of looming fate, bewilderment, and paralyzed. Although the individuals

76

who experience the ill effects of this issue feel weakened, it is one of the most workable disorders to treat using cognitive-behavioral therapy.

When people initially seek cognitive-behavioral therapy, they may show that they have gotten earlier counseling, have made endless visits to specialists, and have been treated in crisis centers for symptoms related to their anxiety. Patients are generally anxious to get answers to ease their on-going battle with panic.

Patients are relieved to realize that their symptoms are treatable using cognitive-behavioral therapy. Frequently, patients feel that they are going crazy, although they should be consoled that having "crazy" feelings is a cognitive bending and is inconceivably different from the individuals who may be viewed as clinically crazy.

Most people know the time-frame when they previously began encountering panic attacks. There may have been activating occasions that cultivated the rise of panic. The patient might be not able to make a connection between the fear and painful triggering experience. Factors, for example, include a significant ailment, work pressure, family abuse/injury, losing a friend or family member, and lacking enthusiastic emotion may make conditions ready for a panic attack. When a panic attack occurs, further attacks usually follow if an individual doesn't know about the cycle of senseless thinking and action, which continues the panic procedure.

The way to shortening a panic attack is to help people comprehend that it's the optional symptoms that keep the fear alive. As it were, it's the "panic over the panic" that continues the panic pattern. With cognitive-behavioral therapy, recuperation includes teaching the sufferer about approaches to respond to their pointless way of thinking during the beginning of their attack. For instance, suppose that you are taking a mid-term test during school. You open up the test booklet and promptly respond by saying, "Goodness my God, none of this material looks commonplace; it is highly unlikely that I can breeze through this test; if I fail this test, I may bomb this course for the semester; if my folks discover, there will be hell to pay!"

Interestingly, you can figure out how to respond rationally by saying, "Fabulous, a portion of this stuff doesn't look familiar; I need to simply take some deep breaths and unwind; I guess I better look over the entire test, answer the questions that I can and afterward return and work on the other ones; I can handle this test, I simply need to unwind and be patient!"

How one responds to panic decides if it dies down. The individuals who battle with their fear by "awfulizing" about their symptoms, intensify their panic. They may state, "Goodness my God, here come those agonizing feelings again - I have an inclination that I'm going to die!"

However, the individuals who acknowledge their panic and respond rationally with contemplations like, "Here comes that panic again - quiet down and take those deep breaths and it will, in the end, die down. These feelings won't keep going forever; they are time-restricted - they'll be gone soon."

Learning through cognitive-behavioral therapy to go "downstream" with panic is imperative to its destruction. The individuals who "catastrophize" about their symptoms intensify panic attacks. Figuring out how to rationally respond to fear lessens its impact. Attempting to make sense of what caused a person's panic isn't essential to treat it. What is fundamental is encouraging the individuals who experience the ill effects of fear to respond with positive self-talk.

People who experience panic attacks will, in general, feel embarrassed about their concern. It is significant for sufferers to comprehend that they are not the only one - anxiety is separated from the human condition. Anxiety and panic aren't uncommon, and the individuals who experience it have to figure out how to be increasingly open and expressive with the majority of their feelings.

Offering a full scope of emotions to those you can trust is fundamental to the healing process. The individuals who hide panic as a disgrace-based example set themselves up to repeat it. When those we believe know about our true self, which incorporates our helplessness, our anxiety issues will end up blurring into insignificance.

Astonishing intercessions can be useful in managing the panic issue. Having a patient calendar, a panic time and urging them to perseverate can acquire diversion and help to break the panic cycle. A pondering patient may be approached to guide breathing exercises during panic-related chest tightness to try to improve the moment and break the cycle of misery.

Cognitive-behavioral therapy is an organized, sober-minded methodology which helps people anticipate the symptoms of panic by figuring out how to respond to the turmoil with a constructive way of dealing with their thinking.

CHAPTER SIX
CBT IN THE TREATMENT OF SEX ADDICTION

"Men are bothered not by things that occur, however by their sentiment of the things that occur." Epictetus (c. 50 - 120)

The philosophical reason for psychological therapy returns to the Stoic Philosophers who taught that it isn't the external occasion that causes our trouble, but instead our recognition or translation of the event that is upsetting. As indicated by the Stoics, individuals are right for considering elective observations or understandings by changing the thoughts that underlie the trouble.

Intellectual models ended up prevalent in the mid-1960s. Defenders of this school accept the client's problems happen at two levels. The first is the apparent difficulty, for example, depression or sex addiction. The second includes tending to fundamental mental components and subjective psychological twists, as a rule including silly beliefs that cause the addictive behaviors.

Subjective behavioral treatments conceptualize mental problems fundamentally as far as maladaptive learning and are arranged toward helping the person to adapt progressively versatile examples of thinking and acting. This technique depends typically on mediations that are ordered, useful, task-oriented, and educative.

It is critical to comprehend the cause for finding intelligent ways to deal with treatment: the apparent problem (sex addiction) begins inside what psychological behaviorist call the client's schemata. This is an individual's reality view or core belief framework.

The focal points of this methodology are on how the client keeps up distressing, unsafe, or silly behaviors. The essential method uses some discussion. This includes bringing up to clients the madness of specific contemplations, beliefs and observations and the development and practicing of sane self-proclamations or other progressively utilitarian subjective procedures and skills.

My center, when working with a subjective model, incorporates:

1. The attention is on halting the undesired sexual intercourse behavior. Potentially pharmacotherapy or Behavioral modification techniques (Relapse Prevention Skills) are utilized to enable clients to develop patience.

2. This is the "affirmation" arrangement and requires the patient to acknowledge the presence of a problem and to guarantee to stay discreet from the specialist.

3. In this stage, patients are shown pressure management techniques, so they never again need to depend on sexual behavior to ease their restlessness. I prescribe physical exercise and present a mix of breathing techniques, hypnosis, self-motivated relaxation, and reflection to indicate to clients that they do have some

control over their inward states.

4. This might be the most significant phase of the program. It comprises of intellectual therapy coordinated towards revoking the silly beliefs that underlie sexual addiction through dynamic addressing. It enables clients to build up a consciousness of ideas. By posing inquiries, clients form an understanding into their point of view and how this impacts their feelings and behavior.

Appropriately the client winds up mindful of unseemly beliefs and has tested them and changed their behavior. The process includes posing inquiries that help or invalidate the idea, getting some information about conceivable elective clarifications. Addressing the scope of results of the concept and it's the effect upon the individual and what might be the impacts of accepting the idea or of changing their reasoning.

5. Patients are prepared in such skills as confidence and problem gauging to encourage versatile social functioning.

6. The concentration is on settling whatever problems the individual has had in building up and keeping up an essential sexual relationship.

7. Realizing what manners of thinking lead to "setting oneself up" for an arrival to fail.

8. Building up an inspirational demeanor towards solid sex; developing gratefulness for the needs of one's partners, getting the hang of pleasuring skills, utilizing sex therapy if there is sexual problems.

9. Producing enjoyable peaceful exercises and connections - building a life worth living.

The sex junkie relies upon sex to meet his enthusiastic needs, which he can't achieve through solid adapting skills. Sex turns into a way of dealing with stress for managing pressure, disgrace, blame, and separation. It is an approach to an interface without risking closeness.

Be that as it may, the addiction is perpetually discontent since sex can't address these issues because their source is authentic and the need is excessively incredible. Moreover, the needs of the genuine self can never be met by sexual activity.

Patrick Carnes sets out the oblivious belief systems that all sex addicts need to disprove.

1. I am primarily an awful, disgraceful individual.

2. Nobody would love me as I am.

3. My needs are never going to be met if I need to depend on others.

4. Sex is my most significant need.

While this is the core dysfunctional ideas, there are so many more beliefs, frames of mind, or "subjective construction" that keep the addictive cycle set up. From my experience, some of them are:

I can't endure boredom; sexual carrying on is a decent method to fill in the time.

If not occupied by sex, I am loaded up with an unbearable feeling of vacancy.

Men are more sex-driven than ladies. As a man, I need to release that drive, or I'll go insane.

My feeling of self is dictated by what number of ladies are attracted to me.

The changes in life are either exhausting or unmanageable. There is no delight to be had in everyday life aside from my "mystery" world.

Sex with my partner is a mechanical, stifling process which needs suddenness and energy.

If life does not provide passion and high-incitement, at that point, I'll be exhausted and discouraged forever.

When I get an inclination or drive to carry on sexually, I should yield to that desire.

With the goal for me to be a real man, I should engage in sexual relations with the most ladies as I can. Besides, as the man, I am in charge of my partner's pleasure through intercourse. Falling flat at sex is flopping as a man.

Taking part in cybersex is my lone methods for heading in the opposite direction from the pressure and dissatisfaction of living.

Sexuality is the main trustable methods for identifying with others.

I rely upon sex to address serious subject matters which I can't meet through sound adapting skills.

Addiction is self-sustaining; it benefits from itself as a result of instilled core beliefs just as everyone has dysfunctional ideas about sex. To change the addictive cycle, one must change the belief systems that underlie it.

Dysfunctional beliefs offer ascent to defense, minimalization, and justification. The fiend, as the ailment advances, sees the world through psychological bends intended to secure his sexual carrying on. His entire viewpoint ends up misshaped to the point where he turns out to be progressively withdrawn from the real world.

In treatment, changing these beliefs is critical. Changing core beliefs is a trial since they were engraved at an early age and have stayed stable after some time. Another reason change that is confusing is that these beliefs live in the unconscious personality. Someone who is addicted needs realization of his reckless ideas. How might you change something you don't realize you have? The independent expert will inspire these frames of mind and beliefs and gives alternate perspectives and views.

Dialectical Behaviour Therapy (DBT) Vs Cognitive Behavioural Therapy (CBT)

Dialectical Behavior Therapy (DBT) is an effective procedure created by Linehan, a brain science specialist at the University of Washington, to treat people with Borderline Personality Disorder (BPD). DBT joins Cognitive Behavioral Therapy with ideas of systems from different strategies, including Eastern mindfulness tactics.

Research has demonstrated that DBT is the first

Therapy that has been effective in treating BPD. Further research has been completed and seems to confirm that it is additionally useful in treating people with a range of state of mind disorders, including self-hurting behavior. Linehan made DBT in the wake of understanding that different treatments were insufficient when utilized for BPD. She perceived that the incessantly self-destructive people she worked with had been raised in invalidating situations and required unqualified acceptance with the goal for them to build up a productive therapeutic relationship. She additionally maintained that people need to perceive and accept their low degree of emotional function and be prepared to make a change in their lives.

Helping the individual with Borderline Personality Disorder to make therapeutic changes in their lives is exceptionally difficult, in any event for two reasons. Right off the bat, concentrating on patient change, both via inspiration or by showing them new conduct skills, is frequently experienced as invalidating by damaged individuals and can accelerate withdrawal, resistance, and drop out from treatment from one perspective, or outrage, hatred, and assault, on the other.

Furthermore, disregarding the requirement for the patient to change (and in this way, not advancing genuinely necessary change) is likewise experienced as invalidating. Such a position does not take the genuine issues and negative results of patient conduct indeed and can, this way, accelerate frenzy, misery, and suicidal ideations.

DBT includes two components:

I.   An individual element in which the specialist and patient talk about issues that surface during the week is recorded on journal cards, and they are used to pursue a treatment target progression. These sessions usually keep going for 45 minutes to an hour and are held weekly. Self-Harming and Suicidal practices take first requirement, trailed by therapy meddling practices.

After this, issues are encompassing personal satisfaction and progressing in the direction of improving one's life in general. During the everyone therapy, both the patient and specialist work to improve skills use to endure and oversee difficult emotions. The entire session ought to progress in the direction of a setting that is favorable for the patient. A great deal of consideration ought to be paid to the quick issues, sentiments, and activities. Frequently, skill group is talked about, and hindrances by acting skillfully is tended to.

II.   The group, which as a rule will meet once per week for two to more than two hours, every seven days, figures out how to utilize specific skills which can be separated into four modules: Interpersonal Effectiveness Skills, Distress Tolerance Skills, Core Mindfulness Skills, and Emotion Regulation Skills.

The room ought to be arranged like a study hall with the coaches (usually two) put at the front. Issues and emotions are talked about and managed if they are life threatening or are interfering with group therapy. For instance, if somebody is carrying on severely, this would possibly be tended to if it was causing an issue with the running of the group. Else, it would be overlooked.

Skills Training is spent around a manual that gives subtleties of the program that must be pursued. This provides direction and counsel about how it ought to be taught. It likewise contains handouts for individuals. Group work can incorporate the imaginary and, as in CBT, homework is energized.

Responsibility - Before DBT can start, the patients need to make a promise to take an interest in the Therapy. This is an activity in itself and may take a few meetings. Both the patient and the advisor have clear responsibilities. Practically speaking, the advisor may at first 'play hard to get' and lead the patient, to induce the person in question that the program is really justified.

People with BPD have regularly experienced medications that have been, best case scenario unrewarding. Subsequent attentiveness should be approved, and the new remedial undertaking displayed sensibly as promising , yet besides requesting — time spent working before Therapy is wise speculation.

In a like manner, if the symbiotic relationship turns out to be unbalanced or takes steps to separate, at that point time should be spent on keeping up this responsibility. It is common for there to be an understanding that if three back to back sessions of one kind are missed in any capacity whatsoever, then the patient is out of the DBT program.

Normal Commitments in DBT

Patient Agreements

- Agree on a time breaking point to remain in Therapy

- Work towards lessening self-destructive practices

- Attend all Therapy sessions

- Participate in Skills Training

Advisor Agreements

- Make a push to direct capable Therapy

- To be moral and professional according to proficient rules

- To look after secrecy

- Obtain consent when vital

- Be accessible for Therapy sessions and back up when required

None of these components are utilized without anyone else's input. The individual element is viewed as essential to keep self-destructive desires or uncontrolled emotional issues from disturbing group sessions, while the group sessions show the skills exceptional to DBT, and furthermore, give work on managing emotions and conduct in a social setting.

The Four Modules

Mindfulness

Mindfulness is one of the center ideas driving DBT. It is the ability to focus, in a nonjudgmental manner, on the present moment. Mindfulness is tied in with living at the time, encountering one's emotions and faculties ultimately, yet with a point of view. It is viewed as an establishment of the different skills taught in DBT because it enables individuals to accept and endure the ground-breaking emotions they may feel when testing their propensities or presenting themselves to disquieting situations. The idea of mindfulness and the thoughtful activities used to teach it are gotten from traditional Buddhist practices. However, the form taught in DBT does not include any religious ideas.

Relational Effectiveness

Relational reaction examples taught in DBT skills training are fundamentally the same as those illustrated in numerous decisiveness and relational critical thinking classes. They incorporate effective methodologies for requesting what one may require, figuring out how to say no, and adapting to relational conflict.

Individuals with Borderline Personality Disorder as often as possible have excellent relational skills in a general sense. The issues emerge in the use of these skills in a specific situation. An individual might almost certainly portray lively behavior groupings when talking about someone else experiencing a dangerous situation, yet might be unequipped for producing or completing a comparable social arrangement when dissecting his or her position.

The relational effectiveness module centers around cases where the goal is to change something (e.g., mentioning that somebody accomplishes something) or opposing changes another person is attempting to make (e.g., saying no). The skills taught are proposed to boost the odds that an individual's objectives in a specific situation will be met, while simultaneously not harming either the relationship or the individual's sense of pride.

Emotion Regulation

Individuals with Borderline Personality Disorder and self-destructive individuals are habitually emotionally dangerous and labile. They can be furious, seriously baffled, discouraged, or on edge. This recommends these customers may profit by assistance in figuring out how to direct their emotions. Persuasive Behavior Therapy skills for emotion guideline include:

- Identifying and naming emotions
- Identifying hindrances to changing emotions
- Reducing helplessness to emotion mind
- Increasing positive emotional occasions
- Increasing mindfulness to current emotions
- Taking inverse activity
- Applying distress tolerance systems

Distress Tolerance

Numerous present ways to deal with psychological well-being treatment center around changing distressing occasions and conditions. They have given little consideration to accepting, discovering significance for, and enduring distress. This errand has, for the most part, been handled by psychodynamic, psychoanalytic, gestalt, or account treatments, alongside religious and profound networks and pioneers. Argumentative conduct therapy stresses figuring out how to tolerate torment skillfully.

Distress tolerance skills establish a symptomatic improvement from mindfulness skills. They have to do with the capacity to accept, in a non-evaluative and nonjudgmental design, both oneself and the present situation. Although this is a nonjudgmental position, this does not imply that it is one of endorsement or renunciation.

The objective is to wind up able to handle the perceived negative situations and their effect smoothly, as opposed to becoming overpowered or escaping them. This enables individuals to make intelligent choices about whether and how to make a move, as opposed to falling into the dangerous, edgy, and frequently ruinous emotional responses that are a piece of borderline personality disorder.

Skills for acceptance incorporate radical acceptance, turning the psyche toward acceptance, and recognizing "ability" (acting skillfully, from a reasonable comprehension of the current situation) and "stiff-necked attitude" (attempting to force one's self will be paying little respect to the real world). Members likewise learn four emergency basic instincts, to help manage prompt emotional reactions that may appear to be overpowering: distracting one-self, self-calming, improving the occasion, and considering upsides and downsides.

Cognitive Behavior Therapy For Anxiety

Cognitive behavior therapy for anxiety is therapy to break the cycle of wrong thinking. It gives an individual back control, as well as instructs, and changes the way particular examples or way of life have been lived.

From adolescence or through horrible accidents, we gain proficiency with a lot of adapting abilities that can progress toward becoming ways of dealing with stress. This kind of treatment has been demonstrated to be immensely affective in treating anxiety and helping patients comprehend why they do what they do and how to change it.

When an individual feels fear, the body will respond as though that fear was genuine. So if you feared that breeze whipping through the trees would make them crash down around you, your body would discharge adrenaline in response to that fear.

Presently if you were completely in danger, that adrenaline could give you a burst of vitality that could cause you to escape from the danger to save yourself. That is a positive response. An undesirable answer is living in anxiety in light of what does not occur. For example, you fear getting terminated. It hasn't happened, yet you worry about it — not a once in a while worry, but rather an all the time worry.

You fear that you will have a mishap while travelling to work. You worry that something may happen to your youngsters, to your folks, to your life partner. You fear

94

that your home may burn to the ground or you may lose every one of your reserve funds. Everybody has passing thoughts where a twinge of worry or anxiety will happen.

That merely is living life on the planet we live in. When the thoughts don't cruise by, when they stick around in our psyches, and we play them over again like a broken record, that flags an issue. Cognitive behavior therapy for anxiety encourages the psyche to quit playing that broken record and causes sufferers to move past the spot they're trapped in.

Therapy and instruction about anxiety and understanding why a few thoughts make an activity and trigger a response can prompt opportunity. The negative self-talk can be changed into positive self-talk. If you set aside the effort to look at a portion of the thoughts you have, you may even perceive how you take similar paths. You were shown growing up or by a horrible mishap.

We, as a whole, have a conviction framework; however, not every one of the things we accept is, in reality, evident. We can change what is great and what is correct and mix it up in our brains with convictions that are hurtful and wrong. Suppose that you have a fear of snakes since you ventured onto one as a kid and it bit you.

You have a chance to visit an aquarium yet don't go because you're stressed that the snakes may escape their pens and you'll get bitten. Notwithstanding, thinking about getting bitten again makes you feel like you're going to blackout. Your heart begins beating fast, and your head starts to throb.

This is a physical response to the fear of what could have occurred, however, hasn't. Cognitive behavior therapy for anxiety can help individuals defeat the stress that keeps them living in fear.

In this example, I think to recall that I am disputing my thoughts to feel better where I am, since I am not at the zoo, or close to any snakes.

What's more, incidentally, fear of snakes is an underlying fear for us people, going way down into the more established pieces of our brain.

In my annoyance the executives directing, I regularly request that customers disclose to me the account of what happened the night they got caught, and frequently a significant number of the feelings related to that occasion will return, and I will intrude on them to ask them how they are feeling, and with a touch of prodding most will almost certainly identify a feeling (frantic, happy, fear, tragic) and I will inquire as to whether the individual, spot, or thing being examined is in the life with us.

The appropriate response is always 'no," so we have a magnificent example of how the thought brings the feeling, for this situation a memory, which might be a programmed negative thought (ANTS).

As one perceives those ANTs, one can venture on them, and the picnic can go on.

Dr. Daniel Amen utilizes the example of ants at a picnic to illustrate how ANTs can wind up dangerous.

He says one or ten ANTS at a picnic will likely not be

an issue. However, twenty or thirty can destroy the picnic.

So how would you contest ANTS?

Initially, one must get familiar with the early warning indications of ANTS, which will be a feeling, specific sorts of words in your thoughts (should, should, must, need to, for example), or behavior, and change the thinking or perception or take a time out.

ANTS can show up in 1/eighteenth second, and the physiology of fear or outrage is direct with the ANT.

If cognitive behavioral therapy for ANTS appears to be inconceivable due to the speed at which your Central Nervous System works, recollect you have been active at your very own adaptation of this a great many times.

Be that as it may, breakdowns can be serious, so figure out how to substitute thoughts like "Appreciation is the Attitude" for ANTS, and you will start the way toward getting more potato serving of mixed greens at the picnic as opposed to tossing verbal or physical punches.

If you are searching for a modern quality device for cognitive behavior therapy for anxiety, you should investigate heart rate inconstancy biofeedback.

Heart rate changeability biofeedback is an electronic program that will give you ongoing criticism about your thinking and how it impacts your body. You can perceive what thoughts of appreciation and thoughts of exploitation do to your heart rate changeability cognizance and how quick that occurs, and train the cognitive antidote to anxiety, by asking the mind in your heart to gain proficiency with another aptitude.

Heart rate inconstancy biofeedback is a quick procedure to adapt; however, look at the recordings in the accompanying link to get a feeling of it.

How To Treat Obsessive Compulsive Disorder – CBT

Step by step instructions to treat obsessive-compulsive disorder relies upon the profundity of the issue. The more time the condition has existed, the more difficult and increasingly imbued it will be. The initial step, in any case, is to identify whether you have an obsessive-compulsive disorder.

We, as a whole, have certain rituals we apply consistently. They can incorporate twofold checking the locks on your home or vehicle, visit hand washing, and molecular characteristics like tapping your pencil multiple times before beginning a test.

For whatever length of time that they don't occupy a significant part of your day, these rituals are futile. Twofold checking of flocks and whether the stove is off are great propensities to get into for apparent reasons. Washing your hands after any occasion that can cause dangerous germs is additionally a decent ritual. Tapping your pocket to watch that you have your keys is additionally a legitimate activity.

'Good Karma' movements are likewise alright when

they are periodic and under specific situations. These may include touching your cap before striking that golf ball, tapping the dash of your vehicle before heading out, or some other silly activity.

What's the Difference Between Obsessive-Compulsive Disorder (OCD) And Just Plain Rituals? The best approach to differentiate obsessive-compulsive disorder from an essential ritual is if you are relaxed. People with OCD will, in general, more than once do something very similar again and again, well past the need. For example, they'll wash their hands once, at that point, do it more than once to persuade themselves they have wiped off the dangerous germs.

The obsessive piece of OCD is brought about by things like fear of germs and soil, fear of disease or damage, envisioning being hurt, fear of losing control, fear of having forceful urges, fear of improper contemplations, and so on.

Impulses are endeavors to free themselves of those obsessive contemplations. The subsequent fixations, for the most part, can incorporate rehashed hand washing, tallying, checking, and touching.

Generally, they're attempting to treat their obsessive propensities by applying compulsive activities. Another strategy they regularly use to self-treat is to self-sedate, which can cause substance-misuse (medications or liquor) issues.

Obsessive conduct like this assumes control over their lives since they never feel they are spotless enough or that they have evacuated the phobias. They invest such a considerable amount of energy in the conduct that they make themselves late for meetings.

A kid may feel the impulse to touch or include every post in a fence the person in question passes. A typical one is doing whatever it takes not to step on the cracks of the sidewalk. These can carry on into adulthood, as well.

When the condition turns into a diversion, it can deliver extraordinary distress and anxiety. Stress can make the situation more terrible.

What Causes Obsessive-Compulsive Disorder? It has been proposed that OCD includes communication issues in the brain, which has been connected to a brain substance called serotonin, which controls brain communications. Deficient degrees of this synthetic is known to be included. Other than this, scientists can't demonstrate any known reason for OCD. They have held up, however, that it can keep running in families.

OCD can take after post-traumatic stress disorder, yet the difference is that OCD isn't explicitly brought about by a horrible occasion like posts traumatic stress disorder. It is additionally easy to recognize from maniacal disorders like schizophrenia and phobias since people with the obsessive-compulsive disorder are entirely mindful of what's genuine and so forth.

They additionally understand that their condition isn't typical. This makes them avoid society since they are humiliated or embarrassed.

Step by step instructions to Treat Obsessive-Compulsive Disorder: Cognitive Behavioral Therapy at one time, nobody realized how to treat the obsessive-compulsive disorder. Cognitive-behavioral therapy is currently known to be the appropriate response. Intriguing to take note of that cognitive-behavioral therapy is additionally now it's generally used to treat anxiety and frenzy. This makes it the perfect treatment for people who are obsessive-compulsive and on edge.

While meds to support the serotonin levels will mitigate the manifestations, cognitive behavioral therapy will cause intense enhancements in the long term.

Cognitive-behavioral therapy includes reinventing the brain, so it winds up desensitized to those fearful contemplations and situations. It instructs the people to substitute methods for handling the stresses, phobias, misgivings, stress, and anxiety in their lives.

You have to discover somebody who realizes how to treat the obsessive-compulsive disorder. A cognitive-behavioral therapy pro ought to be looked for because they'll comprehend the condition and precisely what you're experiencing and will know how to enable you to conquer it.

Each individual group has neighborhood psychological well-being masters, specialists, analysts, and advisors who are preparing correctly in how to treat obsessive-compulsive conduct. Begin with your primary care physician, and he will probably decide the correct way for you. It may be essential to obtain his directions if serotonin therapy is required.

Here is one far-reaching program that gives total directions on the best way to defeat anxiety and related conditions, for example, OCD by utilizing cognitive behavioral therapy.

CHAPTER SEVEN
ENERGIZE YOUR THERAPY SESSIONS - SEVEN PEARLS FOR CBT

Findings have demonstrated that by distinguishing our twisted musings and convictions, we can have better authority over contemplations, and subsequently good control on our sentiments. Having distorted thoughts or feelings doesn't imply that there is something amiss with us. We, as a whole, have changed thoughts and beliefs at different times in our lives. A few instances of distorted thoughts:

OVER-GENERALIZING: At times, we may consider things to be win or bust. For example, if one thing turns out badly with an undertaking, we may believe that the whole venture is a disappointment. Or then again, if there is one thing that upsets us about an individual, we may choose we couldn't care less for that individual by any means.

MIND READING: We expect that we comprehend what somebody is thinking. We may reveal to ourselves that somebody supposes we are "dumb" or dislikes us even though there is no proof that supports this thought. This is called mind reading.

CATASTROPHIZING: We misrepresent how

"horrendous" something is or envision the most noticeably awful conceivable result. Maybe our supervisor needs to talk to us, and we catastrophize that we will be terminated. Or then again, it rains on one of the times of an excursion, and we think "this is the most exceedingly terrible thing that could have occurred."

FORTUNE TELLING: We think we know without a doubt what will occur. For instance, we let ourselves know, "I realize I am not going to get that advancement" or "I won't most likely handle that task."

What's more, specific behaviors or skills are instructed, including social skills, decisiveness, authoritative skills, and unwinding strategies. These are taught during and between sessions.

The following, are seven tips that I will impart to you that I have discovered supportive throughout the years in my practice:

1. Request FEEDBACK

Towards the end of the session, ask what went well during the meeting, what could have gone better, and what the first remove messages are. This fabricates the collusion, improves future sessions, and amplifies progress.

2. Allot HOMEWORK

Towards the end of every session, a collective discussion about activity undertakings" to perform between sessions. An action task may be to purchase a schedule if one of the issues is the time management or recording thoughts and pictures that happen during distressing periods on a notepad to discuss and address at the next session. Continuously make a point to catch up on the home-work or activity task at the next meeting or it gives the feeling that taking a shot at issues or goals in the middle of sessions is anything but a critical piece of showing signs of improvement.

3. Remain FOCUSED

Toward the start of treatment, goals for therapy are discussed. Sometimes, the therapy session may travel toward a path that is inconsequential to any of the goals of treatment. This is proper at specific times, yet if this is occurring each session and for the whole term, at that point, there can be a cutoff to the progress of therapy. The structure is significant in CBT, yet adaptability is likewise substantial. This would be a time to team up to discuss whether to proceed on the present redirection or issue that is being considered or return to what was found in the plan.

4. USE FLASHCARDS

Cheat sheets can be utilized to recall the critical purposes of the session or a mantra that may help with specific thoughts or emotions. If I am working with a patient who is battling with sorrow, I will title the cheat sheet something like "Survival Kit," and it will include methodologies to adapt to the downturn, for example, connecting with a companion, escaping the house, contacting me, or dealing with a little errand.

5. DISCUSS WHERE TO ADDRESS THE ISSUE

Most therapy goals will have a few segments, including distorted thoughts, beliefs, or behaviors. In this way, during the session, cooperatively settle on which level to address the goals. If you are taking a shot at distorted thoughts, it is critical to evoke what ideas or pictures happen that are prompting the pain, for example, nervousness, low mind-set, or hindering a specific behavior.

If you are taking a shot at particular actions, for example, social skills or relationship issues, it is essential to discuss when the skills will be utilized and how likely it is the skills will be used. Another valuable method for addressing behaviors is imagining and envisioning, which practices the skills and address any squares or tensions around the response.

6. Begin EACH SESSION WITH AN AGENDA

Each session should begin with a motivation that is discussed cooperatively between the advisor and the patient. Once more, this keeps the course engaged and increasingly viable. The motivation ought to include following up on homework from the previous session, a registering about the state of mind and week, crossing over or auditing the points and progress of the prior course, and subjects identified with discussing in the present session that is identified with a specific goal.

7. DISCUSS GOALS OF TREATMENT

During the underlying appraisal stage, it is imperative to work together on the goals of treatment. This helps keep the treatment engaged and beneficial. Without goals, therapy can wind up concentrating on whatever issue is coming up that week and can meddle with the progress of the first introducing issues.

Sometimes, the patient will be unable to accurately depict a goal aside from an unclear "I need to be less restless" or "I need to feel more joyful." This is fine toward the start. Be that as it may, over the first couple of months, you should come back to this discussion about goals to check whether they can be depicted in progressively specific terms.

For instance, if somebody presents with melancholy, the goals may include the accompanying: Finding an all the more satisfying activity, coming back to school, practicing three times per week, making two new friends, and stop smoking marijuana.

Psychological, behavioral therapy is an incredibly successful type of treatment, either with or without meds and is an astounding method to practice psychiatry.

CBT And Depressive Ruminations

Cognitive Behavioral Therapy, or CBT, is a viable mental treatment for a full scope of psychological and passionate issues. As a specialist in Edinburgh, I use CBT techniques broadly. I likewise observe many customers experiencing depression. A noticeable component of their side effect profile is the nearness of "Depressive Ruminations."

The expression "rumination" identifies with a

rehashed cycle of action - on account of dairy animals ("ruminants"), this implies chewing the cud! In CBT circles, ruminations are the repeated, apparently perpetual, "stuck" ways of thinking found in certain mental conditions. It is especially common in depression.

There can be many "subjects" to a people rumination, yet the most common is a quest for a type of answer to addresses, for example, "Why am I feeling this way?" or "What might I be able to have done to dodge this?". Another common subject is one of regret or lament - "If just I had done (whatever) differently I wouldn't be in this position now" or "I've destroyed my life." Depressive ruminations about what's to come are likewise observed - "Everything will turn out badly." Ruminations frequently consolidate what a CBT therapist would call "Thinking Errors."

What does it feel like to ruminate? I'm confident we've all done it at some time! It resembles attempting to explain an unsolvable question - you go all around inside your head, analyzing a similar old "clues," time and time once more. If just you'd done this, or said that, or had this, or not had that. You persuade yourself that there's an answer and that when you think that it is, then you'll be fine. There is no "answer." Individuals can ruminate for quite a long time in severe cases, yet as long as an hour is increasingly common.

How would you realize when you're ruminating? Since you've quit doing everything else! You haven't turned the page of your book for as far back as 20 minutes, or you're remaining in the kitchen with a dishcloth in your grasp, looking off into space. If somebody asks you what you've been thinking, you can wager it's a similar old, depressive contemplation that you've been bearing for a long time.

Is there an issue with ruminating? All things considered, yes. It differs from different types of the idea, for example, critical thinking, or reflecting, or recollecting, in two ways. Right off the bat, a great many people discover it rather horrendous.

Similar old stress getting beat up over and over will undoubtedly make us feel dismal or on edge. Also, rumination will in general exacerbate (or if nothing else look after) depression - if you focus on how terrible you feel and how sad (you think) your circumstance is, at that point, you will disregard open doors for change.

CBT hypothesis considers depressive to be as a noteworthy deterrent to recuperation from depression, and in that capacity, it is significant for customers to figure out how to manage them. There is a scope of techniques. However, the ones I support as a CBT therapist in Edinburgh are both straightforward and viable (and practical common sense!).

If you understand you are ruminating, at that point, now's the time to accomplish something vigorous. It's challenging to contemplate when you're out on a run, or swimming, or doing push-ups. The agony will, in general act as a burden! Or on the other hand, if you're not the activity type, take a stab at refocusing your consideration. Focus (truly focus hard!) on some part of your environment - an image on the divider, a tree, the feline - and analyze it for details, taking note of every single abnormality and shade of color.

Imagine that you're a renowned craftsman and that you're going to paint the most beautiful, nitty-gritty, lifelike picture ever! Truly focusing on things outside of you (signifying "outside of your head"!) removes your thinking from ruminative examples.

The last strategy - one that a few customers swear by and others can't get the hang of by any stretch of the imagination - is to "remain back" ("in your head", so to speak!) and let your musings mostly stir away to themselves, while recognizing them as silly manifestations of your depression. By giving them "a chance to get on with it," and declining to "play with them," you break them of their depression-causing ability - in the long run, they'll get exhausted and leave!

The above techniques are those that I've discovered best while filling in as a therapist in Edinburgh. There are various strategies out there in writing, and I don't guarantee that these work for everyone. Something worth being thankful for about the CBT ethos is that it avoids doctrinal doings - there's no "You need to do it along these lines or disaster will be imminent!" in CBT. So the main concern is, utilize whatever technique you discover encourages you the most, and state "Farewell!" to those disagreeable ruminations!

Cognitive Behavioral Dream Therapy: How To Use Your Dreams To Solve Your Problems

Psychotherapists utilize a variety of apparatuses, systems and hypothetical models to support their clients and their patients.

A portion of the approaches we utilize can be moderate, awkward and sometimes ineffectual.

With changing social insurance laws and rising human services costs, specialists should be progressively increasingly productive and increasingly successful in the manners in which that they treat people.

As a major aspect of my preparation and as consequence of numerous years of experience, I have been presented to various different strategies for helping people to change with the goal that they can live all the more satisfying lives.

I am continually searching for straightforward and simple to execute approaches that can help people to develop and to change all the more rapidly,

Presently, there is certifiably not a straightforward solution for each mental, passionate and interpersonal problem. Also, numerous problems are very muddled. Besides, a few clients present with a huge number of problems all the while.

Nonetheless, I have as of late have begun working with

a straightforward model which many individuals appear to discover be very useful.

This approach urges people to utilize their positive and idealistic dreams, daydreams and fantasies to encourage significant changes in their lives.

Cognitive Behavioral Therapy

For a long time, specialists, clinicians, social laborers, marriage and family advisors and emotional wellness laborers have used a triangular model which includes the person's thoughts, feelings and behaviors. These three components sway one another and transforming one variable can regularly encourage changes in another. This model of treatment is known as cognitive behavioral therapy.

CBT, as it is known, centers around changing a person's broken thoughts, or mutilations and nonsensical convictions with the goal that they would then be able to change their feelings and behaviors.

The thought behind this model is that it isn't occasions that disturbed people, but instead their frame of mind and recognitions about the occasions which cause them to be vexed. CBT encourages a person to build up a more advantageous way of thinking about living and about overseeing pressure.

There is much research to help the estimation of this approach and it has been very prominent for around thirty years.

It ought to be noticed that a few people change their

feelings or their behaviors and after that change their thoughts. For example, someone who needs to get in shape may begin a day by day walking scheme and this behavioral shift may make this individual experience a change in the manner they think, as well as the manner in which they feel about themselves and their body.

Since changes in behaviors, feelings or thoughts are very significant in the realm of psychotherapy; it doesn't really make a difference in what manner these changes happen. The primary concern is that people develop, learn and make modifications which enable them to feel much improved and they can function better.

Everything Worthwhile Begins With A Big Dream

One important component that is absent from the daydreams, cognitive-behavioral model is the person's positive dreams, better identified with the arrangement of their showing problem and to the changes that they may need to make in their life.

The new model that I have created starts with an investigation of positive, however reasonable fantasies, since I accept that everything advantageous frequently starts with a person's dream.

For example, a person who needs to open a café may invest a great deal of energy dreaming about the name of the foundation, the stylistic layout and the menu. The future proprietor of the eatery likely envisions oneself walking around the foundation, collaborating with clients and directing the staff and the task of the kitchen.

These components structure the person's dream for his

or her endeavor. The previously mentioned components are most likely important and significant for this business visionary. What's more, the person presumably has invested a great deal of energy picturing what the café will resemble.

Also, dreams like these enable people to connect with their deepest needs, expectations and wants and they urge people to participate in far reaching thoughts and in inventive problem understanding that their cognizant personalities frequently don't enable us to do.

To more readily comprehend this model, think about a square. The upper left-hand corner of the square starts with the person's positive dreams, expectations, wishes and fantasies about how an answer for their problem would look and believe and how it would affect their life.

The rest of the corners can dedicate to thoughts, feelings and behaviors. To put it plainly, I have changed the triangle portrayed before into a square by including one greater component in the fantasy area.

Since certain people don't review their nighttime dreams, they can utilize a fantasy or a dream they have encountered while driving in their vehicle, while driving to work, while running, while at the same time walking, while in the shower, while at work, while tuning in to music or while doing tasks. The greater part of us have daydreams at different times during our everyday exercises and we can without much of a stretch access these important encounters.

Utilizing Your Dreams To Solve Your Problems

So, here is the way this model works. Some of you will most likely utilize this approach without anyone else. Others may require somebody to control you through the procedure.

i. Portray your problem. Begin with one issue at a time.

ii. At that point draw a square. In the upper left-hand corner of your square, compose the word " my fantasy."

iii. In the following three corners think of one of these words, my behaviors, my attitudes, my feelings.

iv. Presently, begin via cautiously thinking about your best dream, daydream or fantasy which incorporates an answer for this problem. Envision how your life will be different once the problem is gone, limited, decreased or lessened. Invest some energy getting a charge out of this charming perspective.

v. Think about what dispositions, behaviors and thoughts you have to change, modify or adjust to enable your dream to turn into a reality. And afterward just move to different corners of the square in any way that you like. Some of you will begin with thoughts. Some of you will begin with feelings and some of you will start with behaviors. Attempt to think of three changes. These changes can be enormous or little.

Return to your square in a week and audit how you are getting along, how you are advancing and how you are feeling.

One of my clients, a dental specialist, brings his square with him constantly. He says it keeps him concentrated on the most proficient method to tackle his problems and how to deal with his life.

Principles of Cognitive Behavioral Therapy

Cognitive-behavioral therapy, or CBT, is a psychotherapy technique that endeavors to teach patients to correct enthusiastic and behavioral responses to disturbing situations. The treatment centers around identifying the circumstances that lead to negative feelings and behaviors, and after that looking at the manner of thinking and beliefs of the patient that leads them to settle on the wrong behavioral choices.

When patients know that they are deciding on the off-base choice and get why they can be retrained to settle on the correct decisions with the outcome being the end of the negative behavior, this is consistently the objective of CBT: to dispose of the negative behavior.

The treatment is powerful when it is done as a deliberate procedure, and it requires some investment. Patients need to experience problem situations on various occasions to have the chance to retrain their reasoning and in this manner, change their behaviors. Cognitive-behavioral therapy has been fruitful in the treatment of dietary problems, nervousness, sleep deprivation, burning chronic disorder, and post traumatic distress disorder.

Cognitive-behavioral therapy had its beginnings in the 1960s when advances in behavioral therapy, which had been around since the 1920s, was joined with the new field of cognitive therapy. The two techniques had their potentials and shortcomings, yet consolidating the two appeared to be the best of the two universes. For whatever length of time that the patient had significant cognitive capacities to comprehend the underlying assumptions that were in charge of their negative behaviors, at that point they could be retrained to evaluate the situation all the more correctly and produce a different feeling or behavior as a response instead of the negative one.

Every individual makes their very own one of a kind view of some random situation. This view is situated to a limited extent on our past encounters as other ecological elements. For specific individuals, this view is contorted, and that leads them to an unreasonable response to the situation. Given their misshaped light, this response may appear to be superbly worthy. Along these lines, the initial phase in cognitive behavioral therapy is to teach individuals to view the inconvenience situations plainly so they would then be able to become familiar with the correct fitting response.

This methodology which legitimately connects with the patient's behaviors is as a glaring difference to the psychoanalyst's approach like that spearheaded by Freud.

Freud's techniques look in reverse, looking out for the base of the issue, while cognitive-behavioral therapy anticipates the final product and begins there. The hypothesis is that if you kill the manifestations, at that point, you have successfully relieved the disorder. CBT expects redundancy to teach patients the suitable responses to improvements and to enable them to see how to settle on that correct choice so they can apply those new essential leadership aptitudes to certain situations.

Along these lines, cognitive behavioral therapy owes an obligation to early behavioral analysts like Ivan Pavlov who among his numerous trials demonstrated that dogs could be prepared to salivate at the sound of a ringer if the music was over and over related with their supper time. Similarly, positive behaviors are developed in patients until that ideally turns into their typical response rather than the negative action that brought them to therapy in the first place.

For the therapist, the way to taking care of a patient's behavioral issues lies in revealing the underlying assumptions that the patient holds that go about as a trigger for the behavior. When the therapist has identified these faulty assumptions, they can help the patient change them. When the patient comprehends that the assumptions they held weren't right, they can be supplanted with correct ones. When this change happens, the patient's responses to situations will likewise change, and the negative, improper behavior will be dispensed with.

Given the sorts of assumptions or even core beliefs that the therapist is posing the patient to review and eventually change, the situation can generally be very unpredictable. Consequently, these techniques require some serious energy. A therapist does not have any desire to shake a patient's belief profoundly without giving them another thing to expand upon so the therapist must move gradually in steps.

Legitimacy testing is a typical initial step, where the patient is approached to clarify or shield his or her beliefs or assumptions. If they are defective, at that point, in the end, the patient will see the imperfections in the rationale. The therapist can't just tell the patient this in any case; the patient needs to learn it all alone, so they comprehend it only as they acknowledge it.

The aftereffects of cognitive-behavioral therapy demonstrate that the protracted procedure merits the exertion because at last, it is compelling. That is why cognitive behavioral therapy is the primary treatment for a wide assortment of disorders from bulimia to frenzy disorder.

CHAPTER EIGHT
CAR ACCIDENT INJURY VICTIMS WITH COGNITIVE BEHAVIOURAL THERAPY?

R oad Traffic Accidents happen daily in their thousands. Numerous people are fortunate, and they are minor accidents bringing about minor injuries, for example, whiplash. They all the time continue to make necessary and snappy unsuccessful no charge personal injury guarantees because of the accident.

Despite the enormous number of minor accidents and personal injury guarantees, there are likewise real accidents, which cause significant and, in some cases, damages. Shouldn't something be said about these accidents? They regularly produce related psychological injuries additionally identified with both the effect of the accident on the accident victim's life and their emotions as needs are.

The physical injuries are all the more effectively dealt with the proceeding with advances in restorative procedures. Anyway, the psychological scars of the accident and the resultant low states of mind and tensions are harder to treat and live with.

There are anyway relatively few alternatives for those

suffering psychologically due to the accident and genuine physical injuries that can some of the time happen. The latest improvement in psychological treatments that don't include taking drugs is that of Cognitive Behavioral Therapy.

In the 1960s, Aaron Temkin Beck depicted his new and progressive leap forward in psychological treatments as "turning on the radio." Having utilized the traditional techniques for Freudian Psychoanalysis, before building up his very own speculations and treatment strategies, Beck had turned out to be progressively baffled in the absence of advancement made by his patients. He wound up persuaded that essential issues causing the psychological bombshell were more in the patient's mentality at the time rather than the issue that set off the attitude previously.

To perceive how this treatment could be rewarding to victims of Road Traffic Accidents who have endured psychologically because of the accident, we have to set up the nuts and bolts behind Beck's then-new therapy.

Beck found his hypothesis during one of his sessions when it turned out to be clear to him that the patient's exhibiting issues were not so much the reason for the effect the patient came to see him about, yet more in the present outlook the patient was in.

To utilize a pertinent model, if we have young fellow associated with a genuine street auto collision which has caused critical physical damage, we will perceive how psychological damage could happen. Anyway, much of the time the victim goes onto enduring depression due to not the accident, but instead from the conditions around him and his emotions.

He could not have had the option to work since the accident making his wife need to take on another job, it is this that at that point causes a negative emotion and thoughts like "I am inadequate to be her better half" or "look what I have caused her to need to do" along these lines making a negative emotion of bitterness and after that more profound depression.

In 1979, having built up his speculations and tried them, Beck composed a book "*Therapy for Depression*" which was a milestone message in its time and undoubtedly in his field. It depicted both the signs of burdensome intuition styles as well as offering another way to deal with treating the side effects of depression.

So having set up the nuts and bolts, it is then simpler to perceive how his therapy can help victims of Road Traffic Accidents. The treatment goes through 5 exceptional standards.

1. There is continuously another perspective!

The wife of the man above who supposes he is an awful spouse does not feel that by any means, she is happy he is alive and is thinking about him and helping him on his road to recuperation. She has not once thought a terrible thought of him since the accident.

2. Occasions Don't Cause our Feelings!

It's how YOU manage the occasions and your thought processes from that point. Someone else in a similar accident could be beautiful and be focusing more on getting physically fit than what his wife thought at the time.

3. We, as a whole develop a trademark method for seeing the world!

People think. Naturally, this is how our states of mind are directed. Beck begat the expression, "Negative Automatic Thoughts." These are thoughts that are undesirable emotions and are frequently automatic. Anyway, it doesn't mean it is absurd to expect to prepare your brain to think differently and not enable negative thoughts to influence our daily living styles.

4. It's a Two Way Street!

Unmistakably specific thoughts have all the earmarks of being ready to make positive emotions. If the individual engaged with the Road Traffic Accident feels he is unequipped for lifting an overwhelming shopping bag because of his injury caused by the accident, this will trigger the thought that "I am inadequate" at that point, hence there is a decent shot that he will feel blame and disgrace alongside the theory.

Psychological Behavioral Therapy calls attention to that the impact works BOTH WAYS. As such if I am as of now feeling dismal or discouraged, I am additionally considerably more prone to permit the thought related with those emotions, for this situation the thoughts of blame, disgrace, and deficiencies.

Psychological Behavioral Therapy suggests that because our thoughts, conduct, and emotions are interconnected that adjustments in a single will unavoidably change one of the others. An alteration in Behavior will change your thought procedure, which like this will change your emotions, etc.

5. We are for the most part Scientists on a fundamental level!

People make and settle their theories daily and are continually doing as such without knowing it. Science has an excellent practice and hypothesis or speculations. To make something work, it must have two criteria:

I.   It must be predictable with every single accessible datum

II.   It can be tried so we can see if it is trusted or not.

Cognitive Behavioral Therapy works in precisely along these lines by exhibiting to the equivalent to the patient. The victim of the Road Traffic Accident has the hypothesis that since he can't lift that substantial package for his wife, he is inadequate because of the personal injury he received in the Road Traffic Accident and his wife concurs with you. This way then incites Negative Automatic Thoughts and makes the individual burdensome.

If anyway he tried the theory he has quite recently put to himself which set off the thoughts he would soon rapidly come to find that in reality his wife has no such sentiments and was contemplating internally "I'll get this as I don't need his back to get awful again which will make him despondent and in agony."

124

So, this is it. Truly CBT is an extraordinary achievement, and lamentably very regularly people go untreated for their condition when with a modest quantity of straightforward treatment their suffering would benefit from outside assistance. Numerous Personal Injury Practitioners who manage claims for personal injury currently perceive the advantages to an ever-increasing extent and are using the accessible restoration sources throughout the case available to them from safety net providers to help their customers in the recuperation procedure. Lengthy may it proceed, and those suffering peacefully can continue onward with their lives but physically harmed yet rationally upbeat.

Treatment Modalities and Therapies

A panic attack is an all of a sudden showing up the fit of fear, which typically doesn't last over 30 minutes. Ladies develop panic attacks about twice as much as men. An affected person sees an entire arrangement of physical symptoms which are felt by them as life-threatening. Consequently, harassed persons build up a constant fear of the presence of the panic attacks, and they stay away from spots and situations in which they fear to panic.

Panic attacks become evident in 4 areas. If you are affected, you may feel symptoms like these:

i- In the physical area

The blood pressure rises, the breathing gets quicker. A few people get feeble in the knees, feel a tingling sensation in the legs. Everything ends up obscured to them; they get dizzy and feel disgusted. They feel as though they have an irregularity in the throat and chest tightness. Looseness of the bowels and urinary incontinence could happen. Different symptoms: quick heartbeat, heart awareness or irregular heartbeat, trembling, dryness of the mouth, breathing trouble, a feeling of suffocation, substantial pain, stomach-throb, hot flashes or shudders, deafness or a general tingling sensation.

ii- In the passionate area

Uneasiness, a feeling of frailty, deadness, assumptions of falsity, fear to lose control, fear of becoming unconscious or to go crazy, fear to suffer a heart attack or to die.

iii- In the psychological area

Affected people could not think any longer and consider things like: "it would be dreadful if... occurred. Surely I will fall, I will get dizzy, I will get a heart attack..."

iv- In the conducting area

Tormented people keep away from specific places or go there just in a group. They will hustle away from particular situations; they may drink liquor to assemble boldness or take a tranquilizer.

Reasons for panic attacks

Different causes can take cover behind anxiety attacks:

Stress situation:

People who suffer from panic or anxiety attacks are regularly in difficulty or in a crisis for which they find no plan. This could be for example a money problem, a detachment, a loss, a rejection or a grave unending ailment of a relative. Affected persons have a hyperactive sensory system. They respond to neural upgrades significantly more extreme than others and become accustomed to new boosts more gradually than others.

Personality characteristics:

Beset persons frequently request from themselves to do everything impeccably, and they feel in charge of everybody and everything. It is difficult for them to express outrage, and they are not ready as far as possible.

Physical ailments:

Thyroid issues, absence of Vitamin B 1, liver illnesses, an unsettling influence of the calcium balance or infectious disease can, in specific situations, trigger a condition of anxiety. In any case, glucose or low blood pressure can likewise prompt tipsiness, deadness, and sudden fainting. These symptoms could then be misjudged. Now and then, phobias can happen regarding hormonal changes during menopause. Like this, it is reasonable to counsel your PCP or an expert.

Drugs:

There is a scope of medicines which can cause anxiety during the taking of pills or after they stopped taking them, for instance, thyroid prescriptions, antidepressants, antihistamines, specific virus cures, sleeping pills, cardiovascular meds, tranquilizers, and drugs like cocaine or psychedelic drugs.

Mysterious ailments:

Anxiety can likewise emerge regarding psychoses, miseries, and over the top habitual issues.

The course of panic attacks

a. In specific situations, harrowed persons experience bizarre physical conditions like irregular heartbeat, dizzy spells, or attacks of perspiration. This generally happens in a period of physical and additionally, mental stacking. They classify these symptoms as life-threatening and respond panic-stricken. Frequently this occurs at spots where the person has no power over the situation, as at the movies, in a car influx, in the holding up the line, at the beautician, in church, in a retail establishment brimming with people or at events.

b. From that point on, the affected persons are so profoundly shaky by their physical response that they never need to experience this experience again. They start to stay away from the specific situation which they believe is in charge of the major panic attack. They remember this first attack again and again and create, only through a creative mind, a comparative response in the body. The fear of fear emerges. Presently the affected people will utilize a few ways to keep up their day by day schedule. They take a tranquilizer, go out just in groups, begin drinking. They escape from the situations in which their symptoms become evident and pull back from the earth.

c. They begin to accept that they suffer from a grave

disease, for example, a heart shortcoming, an epileptic issue, craziness or even a brain tumor.

Treatment and therapy

These are connected treatments to fix panic and anxiety attacks:

- o Linden Therapy
- o Drugs
- o Relaxation therapy
- o Psychotherapy
- o Cognitive, social therapy
- o Psychoanalysis
- o Psychodynamic treatments
- o Behavioral therapy, especially the introduction therapy

Can A Change In Behavior Help Your Insomnia?

For such a significant number of people, sleep appears as one of the most slippery needs of our time. With a regularly expanding level of time-productive requests, consistent availability to the world, and a web-driven pace, insomnia has turned out to be considerably more pervasive across the globe. This is proven further by the enormous increase in both over-the-counter deals and remedy offers of sleep hypnotics over the most recent two decades. Sadly, practically all of the cures have significant symptoms, a restricted time of adequacy, or all the more critically, a high hazard for reliance for sleep. While meds might be the best for transient insomnia difficulties, long haul insomnia is best tended to by behavioral mediations. This is the place Cognitive Behavioral Therapy or CBT has had a considerable effect in giving enduring relief to my sleep, misfortune sufferers.

CBT fundamentally addresses an individual's behavior by giving instruction and establishing better sleep propensities. Usually, this is given to a person through a few sessions (shifting from 4 to 12) generally lasting around 30 minutes by a qualified sleep proficient. Most usually this is a clinician with uncommon enthusiasm for insomnia, however, nurture experts, doctors, therapists, and others that have direct patient consideration can likewise give CBT if extraordinarily prepared. Simultaneously, misguided judgments and falsehood about sleep, in general, are disposed of, and better sleep hygiene is created.

Regardless of whether weak sleep thoughts are grown instinctively or through different wellsprings of off base data, unfavorable beliefs about sleep can advance and sustain insomnia. For example, a few people may believe that if they hit the hay earlier, they have an excellent chance of getting more sleep. In fact, in any case, this has the contrary impact as hitting the hay earlier declines the possibility of falling to sleep.

This is because the body's circadian musicality, or

everyday bio-mood, has a window of time that is ideal for sleep beginning and attempting to fall asleep outside of this window causes dissatisfaction and anxiety further exacerbating insomnia. Another model is that numerous people may hold a belief that they need at any rate of 8 hours of sleep to feel rested. While most of us need 7.5-8 hours of sleep each night, the range is from 4 hours to 10 hours for different people. If somebody that requires just 5 hours of sleep keeps on attempting to get 8 hours, there can be pointless pressure related to this apparent sleep misfortune.

CBT first targets exact data about a person's sleep and sleep needs and instructs them on verifiable viewpoints about sleep in general. After a point by point, sleep history is obtained, a portion of these errors are uncovered and redressed through discourse and models. At that point at each resulting session, these territories are again talked about to fortify adherence to the recently learned ideas.

Besides, CBT additionally sees general sleep propensities, which usually are alluded to as sleep hygiene. Sleep hygiene depicts gainful behaviors and negative schedules that can influence one's sleep capacity. Areas secured incorporate the sleep condition, sleep plans during the evening, daytime snoozing, measures of invigorating sustenances and drinks devoured, excessively unbending bedtime schedules, general wellbeing behaviors, the timing of activity, and numerous others.

A typical case of this is many sufferers attempt to fall asleep, however regardless of being not able to do as such, keep on lying in bed consistently watching the clock. Positive sleep hygiene urges you to get up following 20 minutes or something like that if sleep isn't obtained, and afterward taking part in a sleep-advancing behavior like perusing.

When you are feeling relaxed once more, another endeavor to fall asleep is attempted. By proceeding to lie in bed, anxiety assembles in this way, making sleep even more unwilling to happen. Indeed, instructing an insomniac about positive and negative impacts of behaviors on rest gives a comprehension after that to change the behavior, therefore establishing a strong therapy for their insomnia.

Insomnia is a condition that in reality, turns out to be progressively regular with age as the mind's components for falling asleep and staying asleep become less potent. What's more, numerous people have a hereditary propensity to be "hyper-alert" and have more prominent difficulty sleeping notwithstanding. Indeed, even in certain insomniacs who do require the supplemental drug for sleep, CBT can give the best format after that these can be viable. Cognitive Behavioral Therapy likewise can identify contemporary issues with misery, anxiety, and other physical problems that may need separate consideration through different measures. If unusual conditions do exist, these should be tended to simultaneously. In such manner, CBT offers the most extensive way to deal with the date for managing insomnia for the long term by giving an foundation of learning and a course for behavior that empowers the insomniac to keep up a great quality sleep.

Therapy Insights in Treating Binge Eating Disorder

One patient managing abuse and injury issues in therapy utilized binge eating to mitigate the indications of sadness and anxiety. As work in therapy proceeded, and it was found that this patient started emotionally eating simultaneously as when the abuse happened. As a kid, certain foods were observed by her parents, for example, oats with sugar. She was just permitted such oats one day out of the week. In this way, the admission of oat on days other than the one previously assigned and additionally if she ate more than a specific sum was observed. As this patient got more established, she discovered that much concentration and consideration was given to what sort of food she ate or did not eat.

When she was not able or was reluctant to verbalize her emotions and feelings, she went on to binge-eating behaviors. It turned into a wellspring of a dispute between the patient and her parents. In treatment, it was found that food was being utilized as a wellspring of getting attention, albeit negative, from her parents. Her parents did not realize she was being abused and, as a kid, she was undermined by the culprit if she informed anybody regarding what was going on. As she got older, when she and her parents did not agree about something, she went to food as a counter against them.

In any case, as she had the option to find and express the hurt and outrage to her parents because specific foods were being observed, she bit by bit utilized different methods for having her needs met. Never again did she have to "rebel" or fight back with food. Instead, she had the option to verbalize the emotions and feelings, and as she did as such, the binge eating behaviors died down.

Work was finished with the parents to enable them to manage their emotions about the abuse too. They felt defenseless and communicated disappointment for not taking care of the injury. In any case, they didn't have any acquaintance with it was occurring. Presently they impart their feelings and assessments straightforwardly.

This contextual investigation demonstrates the significance of tending to the mental issues simultaneously as showing reliable healthful ways of thinking and practices. If just body picture and eating examples were underlined, the dangerous cycle of binge eating would keep on being sustained for quite a long time and go on for years without goals.

The DSM-IV illustrates the qualities and indicative criteria of BED. Numerous patients battling with BED are ashamed about what they are doing and dread others discovering. Therefore, it is useful to know a portion of the pointers of the disorder.

The warning signs of BED are many:

☐ Frequently eating unusual measures of food in a brief timeframe, generally under two hours

☐ Constant weight changes

☐ Not utilizing any techniques to cleanse foods

☐ Rapid weight increase or heftiness

☐ Eating quickly, regularly gulping without biting

☐ Feeling an absence of command over one's eating

☐ Eating alone

☐ Secretive dietary patterns

☐ Hiding or storing food, frequently fatty/"garbage" food

☐ Eating late around evening time

☐ Eating a lot of food without being eager

☐ Disgust and shame with self after indulging

☐ Coping with emotional and additionally mental states, for example, stress, sadness, or dissatisfaction by eating

☐ Attributing one's triumphs and disappointments to weight

☐ Consuming foods to the point of being awkward or even in torment

☐ Avoiding social circumstances, particularly those including food

By and large, these warning-sign behaviors are utilized to comfort and mitigate the person. They are not used as a discipline. As needs are, there are different rewards and battles for the person than the prizes and actions of one battling with anorexia nervosa or bulimia nervosa. The cycle of dependence is additionally different.

Anxiety (works from ruminating considerations and expectation)

Impulsive Behaviors (following up on compulsion - dietary issue behaviors, drugs/liquor, sex, and so forth.)

Essential Difficult Emotion (for example, outrage, hurt, misery, forlornness, and so forth.)

Relief (oft described as "high," "elation" - impermanent because of end of anxiety)

Withdrawal (disengagement, insider facts, and so on.)

Fanatical Thoughts (diverting considerations or fixating on the urgent behaviors)

Optional Difficult Emotions (blame/shame)

For anorexia nervosa and bulimia nervosa, the addictive cycle streams in the way recorded previously. Nonetheless, with binge eaters, the "relief" phase of the period goes before/goes with the enthusiastic behavior of gorging. At that point, they move straightforwardly into the aspect of "optional difficult emotions" and experience what is by all accounts a progressively concentrated self-hatred because of unfortunate social standards about overeating without compensatory behaviors.

Coming up next is a diary portion from a client whose finding was BED, with an earlier conclusion of anorexia. Watch for the situation of the "Relief" period of the addictive cycle in the two passages:

How I feel after I confine:

I believe that I'm beating the beast. I'm defying it. Be that as it may, I think of the vacancy inside me. Possibly I'm intended to manipulate the missing opening. Be that as it may, if this is what not getting what I need is, at that point, what's the end? I might beat the beast, yet longing can develop to an incredible fiasco later. This could be the "right" thing, however. I don't feel humiliated, similar to a pig around others. Be that as it may, my brain is continually considering new things I'm passing up. I'll feel lighter, however, a spring in my progression. No swelling or abundance. Surprisingly better, I may like what my body will resemble.

The section from the binge scene identifies the modified addictive cycle as recently clarified, wherein "relief" goes with the "enthusiastic behavior" rather than coming after the addictive behavior. When a client battles with binge eating, they display different sorts of emotions in both glaring and unpretentious ways. Oft times these patients, if they have a past filled with anorexia or bulimia, will recognize the DSM criteria without unveiling the "warning signs" because of extreme shame.

Feelings and reactions of one battling with BED differ from those of other dietary problems. As needs are, the accompanying intercessions and suggestions help people manage their emotions to determine BED indications and behaviors.

Suitable evaluation as per the DSM-IV criteria, including specific things to represent the "warning signs" as recorded in this chapter. This may elevate anxiety and shame quickly, yet diminishes components that empower the client to harbor shame.

Therapeutic assessment and without up and coming peril center around feelings rather than weight and dieting.

Dieting history, concentrating on serious desiring, crazy feelings with food and the quick and oblivious eating that "dieting mindset" summons. Regularly these are forerunners for gorging finding and feelings of shame are related.

Self-mitigating aptitudes to diminish the power of the initial three phases of the addictive cycle just as give increasingly lasting estimates they gain in the "relief" stage.

Cognitive Behavioral Therapy and Dialectical Behavioral Therapy methodologies give ways to help the client deal with the basic mental ramifications of BED.

We advocate that clinicians, dietitians, and direct-care staff who work with dietary issue patients become mindful of the interesting differences clients with BED understanding so they can be better upheld away from shame and helped into recuperation.

CONCLUSION

S ocial fear is hard to make sense of and can be similarly as difficult to overcome, however, if you can find the underlying driver of your social anxiety you will have a lot more unique possibility of overcoming your social phobia for the last time. This conclusion will help you in your way to recovering your life...

Try not to accept all that you read and hear.

Regularly when an individual experiences social anxiety, they will look for advice and help from companions, family, and many will concede to the Web for information on the best way to overcome social anxiety.

The issue with this technique is that a significant number of the people you will look for advice from have never experienced social phobia themselves and can't identify with what you are experiencing. The web is an excellent spot to find information on overseeing your social phobias, yet there is a lot of terrible information out there so you should sift through and see what works and what does not.

Numerous write-up and sites will give you the equivalent repeated information on how you can overcome social fear, yet most are composed by people who have never endured that tremendous fear of social situations that you are encountering.

I realize how difficult it very well may be to find valuable and significant information because I spent the better piece of a half year looking into and perusing how I could get over my social fear of open talking, meeting new people and the frailties I have about my weight and how people judge me.

How You Got Social Anxiety

No one knows the specific cause for a social anxiety issue. Anyway, numerous medicinal scientists feel that there are three leading causes, including physical, natural, and environmental factors.

Physical - social fear may have been activated from a humiliating moment from quite a while ago.

Organic - social phobia might be the aftereffect of a substance inadequacy with your serotonin levels.

Environmental factors - happens when you witness another person having a mortifying social moment and you fear something very similar transpiring.

Signs of Social Anxiety

While there are numerous signs that you might experience the ill effects of the impacts of social phobia, multiple people frequently don't understand that these manifestations are signs that they are experiencing a psychological sickness and never look for treatment. The most well-known expressions are:

Keeping away from social situations because of fear of being ridiculed, judged, humiliated or mortified

Expanded anxiety or apprehension when in social

situations

Physical manifestations, for example, sweating, becoming flushed, vexed stomach, perplexity, fast beating heart, the brevity of breath, and even looseness of the bowels.

Social Anxiety Treatments

There are three main types of treatment for social phobia, with the correct treatment you can overcome your social fear and carry on with a glad and reliable life, however, in many cases people waste a lot of time in mastering their social anxiety because of tuning in to awful guidance and proposals from other people who have no involvement in managing social fear and are merely offering their opinions.

The key with any tremendous social anxiety treatment plan is to reconstruct your mind by the way it forms your contemplations, feelings, propensities, and behaviors.

I realize this appears to be a lot; however, indeed with the correct preparation and a sound arrangement of attack, overcoming social anxiety is quite a lot more feasible and sensible than numerous people portray it.

Here are the three main types of social phobia treatments accessible:

Cognitive-Behavior Therapy - investigating your psyche and your contemplations and how they influence how you feel in social situations. When you have reinvented your considerations and feelings, you can genuinely begin the path toward overcoming social anxiety.

Prescription anti-depressants, anti-anxiety, and beta-blockers are sometimes utilized in blend with cognitive-behavior therapy to decrease your anxiety levels, however, anxiety prescriptions won't kill your social anxiety long term and once you quit taking them your anxiety returns. There are likewise numerous evil reactions that have been accounted for with these types of drugs.

Neuro-etymological Programming - is among the most potent types of social anxiety treatments accessible. You are finding your capacity covered somewhere inside and getting to the main drivers of your anxiety.